The New Federalism

The New Federalism

Michael D. Reagan

New York   Oxford University Press   1972

To Celeste

Acknowledgments

I am grateful to the students, graduate and undergraduate, whose discussions in seminar helped stimulate this book, and especially to Sheldon Edner, who performed willingly and well as a graduate research assistant. I want to thank, too, Ande Deaver, whose rapid typing enabled me to meet my deadlines.

Contents

I

Prologue

1

Is Federalism Dead?

Federalism—old style—is dead. Yet federalism—new style —is alive and well and living in the United States. Its name is intergovernmental relations.

Old style federalism is a legal concept, emphasizing a constitutional division of authority and functions between a national government and state governments, with both levels having received their powers independently of each other from a third source—the people. New style federalism is a political and pragmatic concept, stressing the actual interdependence and sharing of functions between Washington and the states, and focusing on the mutual leverage that each level is able to exert on the other.

Conventional federalism is a static notion. It pictures the relationship between the national government and the states as something fixed for all time by the founding fathers in 1787. The modern notion of federalism, in keeping with the more realistic approach of present-day political analysis, is dynamic; it pictures the intergovernmental relationship as one of constant change in response to social and economic forces, as well as to changes in such significant political fac-

3

tors as the party and electoral systems. In formal terms, constitutional divisions are changed only by constitutional amendment. In actual political practice, we have long recognized that Supreme Court decisions, Congressional legislation, political custom, and changes in the technology of communications and transportation can all create *de facto* changes in constitutional provisions. The wording of the Constitution is sufficiently broad to cover a variety of situations; thus the form can remain constant while the content changes radically. This is, in fact, what has happened to federalism.

Finally, we have been accustomed to thinking of federalism as an abstract feature of governmental structure. We need to begin thinking of it as a policy determinant. That is, we need to consider its impact upon the day-by-day operations and concrete activities of government—and the reciprocal impact of expanding governmental activities upon the structural relationship between the levels.

The new federalism is better referred to as intergovernmental relations—both because the phrase alerts us to the changed meaning of the concept, and because the cutting edge of federalism lies in the actual (particularly administrative) relationships between the levels of government as they share in the performance of expanding governmental functions. It no longer makes sense to conceptualize federalism as a wall separating the national and state levels of government.

This sharing of functions is most clearly and dramatically seen in the explosive growth of federal grants-in-aid. Such grants—sums of money given by the federal government to lower levels of government in order to finance the performance of specified functions—were estimated at over $30 billion in fiscal 1971; which is more than *quadruple* the amount in 1960. It is on these grants—their origins, purposes, accomplishments, problems, and significance for a political system—and the revenue sharing alternative that this book concentrates, in order to present a realistic picture of the new federalism as we approach the 200th anniversary of the writing of the Constitution.

The sacred triad of American government has always consisted of separation of powers, federalism, and judicial review. In popular usage, each of these concepts has developed its own mythology. In the cases of separation of powers and judicial review, however, political scientists have long since exploded the myths. For example, the conventional wisdom regarding the Supreme Court was the assertion that the judges only interpreted the law; they did not make it or change it. This is how the possession of power by a group of nine men not accountable to the electorate was traditionally defended. In the past quarter-century, historians and political analysts of the Court have made it very clear that the assertion is ridiculous. Such recent landmark cases as *Brown vs Board of Education* (the desegregation decisions of 1954–55), the reappointment cases, and the *Miranda* decision on the rights of a police suspect, make it abundantly clear that the Supreme Court makes law. Similarly, the conventional wisdom on the separation of powers, which holds that the President has no legislative role and the legislature no executive role, has been thoroughly discredited by a generation of research. A leading book on the Presidency now speaks of separated institutions sharing power. This is the realistic picture of Presidential-Congressional relations and it is now pretty thoroughly imbedded in the literature.

Curiously, the revolution in political analysis that has moved away from the study of institutions in their legal forms to the study of realistic political forces and social forces behind them has not been widely extended to the study of federalism. Perhaps because federalism has been seen by political scientists as a structural boundary within which politics operates, rather than as an operative element within politics, they have not paid it much attention. Major exceptions lie in the writings of William H. Riker, the late Morton Grodzins, and Daniel J. Elazar. Riker [1] has examined realistically the origins and conditions of maintenance of federalism, and concludes that a decentralized party system is the essential condition for retaining what he calls "the federal bargain." However, he continues to define federalism in essentially legalistic terms as a matter of dividing decisions between a central government and regional governments in such a way that each has some category of action in which it can make decisions without consulting the rulers of the other level of government. Grodzins [2] and Elazar [3] have made an extremely significant contribution by emphasizing the very extensive degree to which the federal and state governments share in decision making regarding the same functions of government, rather than dividing governmental functions in such a way that each level has its own separate area of action. As Grodzins put it in a now-famous essay,[4] American federalism is not like a layer cake, with each level of government having its own autonomous sphere of decision making; rather, it is like a marble cake, in that decisions regarding a particular function are made at all levels of government, and that all levels typically cooperate in implementing public policies. Like Riker, however, Grodzins and Elazar have improved our understanding of relationships between the national and state and local levels of government without focusing directly on the meaning of federalism. Although this creates a gap through which the conventional myths may continue to escape unchallenged, it may have been a wise decision on their part. When one does try to focus on the meaning of federalism, what one finds is a set of formalistic criteria that may have little real political significance.

That is to say, even when the formal criteria are met, it turns out that we have learned little about the actual distribution of power or functions between the national, state, and local levels of government. It tells us little about the degree of political centralization in a society. The United Kingdom is a unitary state, yet there are important elements of decentralization and regional autonomy. Despite these anomalies, it is the contribution to decentralized political decision making that is usually thought of as federalism's prime value.

The modern classic on the subject of federalism is a book by a British authority, K. C. Wheare,[5] in which he defines the federal principle as "the method of dividing powers so that the general and regional governments are each, within a sphere, coordinate and independent." The modern concept of federalism, he says, has been determined by the USA, where in law the general and regional authorities (i.e. the national and state governments) "are not subordinate to one another, but coordinate with each other." In a viable federalism, according to Wheare, neither level of government must be in a position "to override the terms of their agreement about the power and status which each is to enjoy." The Constitution must be supreme over both levels of government. Discussing the prerequisites of federalism, he adds that the constituent units

> must possess sufficient economic resources to support both an independent general government and independent regional governments. It is not enough that the general government should be able to finance itself; it is essential also that the regional governments should be able to do likewise.[6]

7

As we shall see in some detail, it is exactly the inability of state governments to finance all the services asked by their citizens that has led to the substantial development of federal grants-in-aid, and perhaps now to a true fiscal crisis at the state-local level, especially in the largest cities. As for the proposition that the American states are coordinate with rather than subordinate to the national government, one can only assume that Wheare was not aware of Article VI, Section 2 of the Constitution, which states that national laws are "the supreme law of the land . . . anything in the Constitution or laws of any state to the contrary notwithstanding." By any dictionary, coordinate means "equal in rank or importance." This the American states, vis-à-vis the national government, are not. As a matter of political theory, in addition, it seems dubious that there can be a nation in which there is *no* institutionalized final authority.

In addition to, or in place of, Wheare's criterion of coordinate legal status, there are several other formal attributes of federalism commonly set forth in academic discussions of the subject. These include:

1. There is a constitutional division of governmental functions such that each level is autonomous in at least one sphere of action;
2. Each government is final and supreme in its constitutionally assigned area;
3. Both levels act directly on citizens (unlike a confederation, where only the regional units act directly on the citizens while the central government acts only on the regional governments);
4. Both levels derive their powers from the "sovereign" (i.e. the people or the Constitution), rather than from one another;
5. Therefore, neither can change the relationship unilaterally; and, finally

8

6. The regional divisions (i.e. states) exist as of their own right.

In formal terms, federalism in modern usage is to be distinguished both from *unitary* states, which are those in which all regional and local authority derives legally from the actions of the central government and can be taken away by that government at its pleasure, and, at the other extreme, from mere *confederations* in which the central government does not reach individual citizens directly—as under the 1783 Articles of Confederation.

The formal theory of federalism thus stresses the independence of each level from the other, and the idea that the functions of government are divided so that some (e.g. defense) are exclusively the province of the central government while others (e.g. education, police protection) belong exclusively to the regional units. In the states' rights ideology of federalism in the United States, emphasis has traditionally been placed on two constitutional provisions that are thought to embody the notion of autonomous coordinate entities—the Tenth Amendment and the enumerated powers of the national government contained in Article I, Section 8. The Tenth Amendment states that all powers not delegated to the central government, nor forbidden to the states, "are reserved to the states respectively, or to the people." Article I, Section 8 contains a specific list of powers granted to Congress, such as laying taxes, regulating commerce, coining money, providing an army and navy, and granting copyrights and patents. One strand of popular ideology puts these two segments together and infers that the Tenth Amendment reserves to the states everything not listed in the specific grants of power. A supposedly hard and fast line of demarcation is therefore assumed. This ideology conveniently ignores the so-called "elastic clause," coming at the end of the list of enumerated powers, which states that Congress may "make all laws which shall be necessary and proper for carrying into execution the foregoing powers." Broad construction of this clause by the Supreme Court, defining "necessary" as meaning appropriate to the end and not explicitly forbidden, so effectively expanded the range of subjects on which the Congress could act that the Court came in 1941 to see the Tenth Amendment as simply stating a truism, "that all is retained which has not yet been surrendered." [7] What the judicial doctrine (originally expounded by John Marshall, then backed away from for many decades, and now dominant again) establishes is that the distribution of powers and functions made in 1789 is not sacrosanct, that Congress can unilaterally change that distribution within the very broad limits of what the Court will accept as appropriate means to enumerated ends. Thus judicial interpretation effectively jumps over the formal hurdle of constitutional amendment as the supposed only way by which the division of functions between the levels can be altered. Since the Supreme Court is an instrument of the national government, and the Constitution is—in a famous phrase—"what the judges say it is," the net effect of judicial review is to permit one instrument of the national government to alter the terms of the federal arrangement unilaterally—despite the textbooks. Since the Tenth Amendment has no independent power to foreclose expansions of federal activities under the necessary and proper clause, there is no constitutionally binding permanent division of authority between the national and state governments in the United States.

There are some areas of state action into which the national government has, as a matter of policy, not moved. The law of domestic relations is state law. We do not have national legislation on marriage and divorce—except that polygamy is forbidden. Most of the ordinary legislation affecting property and contracts in business generally is state law rather than national. Since the "constitutional revolution" of the mid-1930s, however, it is perfectly clear that the national government has the authority under the commerce clause to supersede state business law wherever it finds such action to be necessary. While the national government has refrained from pushing its constitutional power as far as it presently could under the elastic clause and under the power to tax and spend,[8] that is a different question from its *legal* ability to supersede state decision making.

It would appear that the only aspect of state government that is beyond the reach of Washington is the very existence of the states with their present boundaries, for the Constitution (Article IV, Section 3) provides that no state may have its boundary changed without its consent. Even the normal processes of constitutional amendment are not legally able to disband a state without its own consent. The governmental structure of the states would seem to be generally a question for self-determination, though even here there is a possibility of national intervention under the clause (Article IV, Section 4) of the Constitution that guarantees to each state "a Republican Form of Government."

The ability of the national government to act in every subject matter area should not, however, be taken to mean that the states have been reduced to nonentities. Although the national government has used its broadened constitutional authority of the past quarter-century to take upon itself many burdens with regard to education, health, public welfare, conservation, and social legislation—all areas once thought to lie within the reserved jurisdiction of the states —its entry into these areas has made it a partner with the states rather than a substitute for the states. Thus a contemporary British observer, M. J. C. Vile, writes that "the foremost characteristic of American federalism . . . is the *inter-*

dependence of federal and state governments, not their mutual independence," and that "Modern American federalism is characterized more by the extent and importance of [an] area of concurrent power, than by anything else." [9] Federal grants-in-aid represent the most significant means by which the national government presently exercises its concurrent powers with the states. We have not in recent years had much of an extension of domestic programs run *directly* by the national government, but we have had a great extension of programs operated by states and localities with federal funds and with varying (though sometimes very substantial) degrees of federal policy control.

The strictest forms of federal control, constituting the highest degree of federal "intervention," do not consist of federal programs replacing national or state activities. Rather, they consist of federal administrative actions, legislation, and court decisions that impose national standards in areas where the previously prevailing community standards were those of the respective states or towns. The most noticeable of these interventions are, of course, those involving civil rights and civil liberties. Decisions by the Supreme Court outlawing racial segregation in public facilities, the Congressional civil rights acts of 1957 and several succeeding years, and executive orders from the President outlawing discrimination in federal employment—which includes federally funded employment through private business contractors—are all examples of national actions taken to make the Fourteenth Amendment to the Constitution a living reality. Similarly, a string of Supreme Court decisions strengthening the rights of defendants in criminal cases and in police work, and in further shoring up First Amendment rights to freedom of speech and expression in such modern forms as the civil rights demonstrations, exemplifies a degree of *national* concern for civil liberties that is undoubtedly greater than would be the concern of many state legislatures or state courts. Citizen participation rights, as reflected in the one man–one vote decisions of the Supreme Court and such legislation as the 1965 and 1970 civil rights acts, with their provisions for compulsory federal voting registrars, constitute also an enlarged area of national standards, with some direct national action.

But note that with the exception of the federal voting registrars, the form that the federal action takes is that of imposing requirements upon either states or private individuals; it does not entail the expansion of the "federal octopus" in terms of either funds or civil servants.

Just as government has learned how to manage the economy as decisively as any explicitly socialist system, yet without engaging in nationalization of the ownership and direct management of plants and factories, so also do we find that the national government can interpose the view of a national majority upon reluctant states and localities, and can strongly influence the budgetary allocations of state governments through the choices it makes in its own grant-in-aid allocations, all without in any way touching the formal structure of federalism. The bottle may be old, but the wine is new. Because of court decisions, custom, and the changing social structure induced by "pictures in our heads" uniformly distributed across the country through the mass media and through the travels of an astoundingly mobile population, we have now arrived at a point in our constitutional history when no sphere of life is beyond the reach of the national government. Since we no longer question the constitutionality of federal acts, the deciding factor becomes one of policy rather than legality. As William Anderson, a close student of the federal system, wrote in 1955,

when Congress considers any new measure . . . it needs to consider carefully whether it is necessary or even desirable to push national action to the limits of national power. In

13

many situations it may be better, as a matter of public policy, to assist and induce the state and local governments to perform the service up to at least a minimum standard.[10]

This is where grants-in-aid play their part: they are the device by which the national government assists and induces state and local governments.

The distance is considerable between federalism conceived as a legal mechanism by which two levels of government are kept at arm's length from one another and governmental functions are neatly parceled out on a "you do this and he will do that" basis, and the idea of federalism as a political dynamic referring to an interdependent and ever-shifting relationship of joint action. In the older perspective, we look upon federalism as a constitutional bulwark against tyranny. Yet Riker argues with some plausibility that the more one believes in freedom the less one can approve of federalism historically in the United States, where its main use has been racial repression. The developing modern perspective views federalism in pragmatic terms as simply a way of getting things done more effectively. From the viewpoint of political science, federalism does indeed have great importance in our system—but that importance does not consist of the original need to compromise between thirteen colonial governments and one central government. Rather, it consists of adding an element of great complexity to political analysis, for in our federal context it becomes a matter for empirical investigation (and reinvestigation because of change) to determine who holds the balance of power and the more influential leverage regarding what each level of government shall do at any particular moment and with regard to any particular subject. In a unitary state, there is less doubt regarding where power lies.

14

The Textbook Picture

To wrench our perspective out of its accustomed angle and refocus it into a better fit with reality is not easy. The difficulty is plain if one looks at any of the basic textbooks in American government. With minor variations, they all just state the formal principles of federalism with a straight face, as it were, and then discuss cooperative shared functions or an actual change in the national-state balance of power without connecting the discussion back to their description of the federalist principle.

Some real inconsistencies or contradictions develop as a result of this bifurcated treatment, for some of the realistic statements of intergovernmental relations clearly violate what textbook authors have earlier presented as the definition of federalism in America. For example, one book cites the founding fathers' notion that each level was to be supreme in its own jurisdiction, yet thirty pages later describes all the changes that had been associated with the shift of power from the states to Washington—without ever pointing out that such changes have vitally affected the original conception. Another recent text even ignores the impact of Supreme Court interpretation of the implied powers clause. It cites as an apparently valid feature of our federal structure that the central government cannot determine which areas it will control because that has been supposedly settled by the Constitution. Occasionally, the effort to fit round pegs into square holes results in rather strained attempts to avoid the recognition of change. Thus one text admits that the national government *appears* to possess powers not recognized in the early years of the nation yet insists that this does not prove that the government exercises more than enumerated powers. Another widely used book in basic

American government courses says that in a "true" federal system, each of the levels of government must be substantially independent of the other; it does not say—despite a whole chapter on modern intergovernmental relations— whether the United States today is or is not a "true" federal system by that criterion. I found just one text that explicitly acknowledges—even stresses—that "over the years, the meaning of federalism has changed." Curiously, the one other text that strongly, although only implicitly, states the great change in the federal relationship is that classic nuts-and-bolts book, Ogg and Ray, the Thirteenth Edition of which argues that development of the grant-in-aid system has made the states into "administrative subdivisions of the national government." [11]

That may slightly overstate the present situation, but it comes a good deal closer to hitting the mark than another textbook which states that "the fact that Congress possesses only powers specifically delegated to it, or reasonably inferred, is one of the outstanding features of American government," and that "being residual in nature, state powers are broader than those of the federal government." [12] I ask the reader: Exactly what powers does Congress not possess under present Court interpretation of the Constitution? If the reader has as hard a time finding any such powers, as I do, why do textbook writers persist in emphasizing an empty formalism?

Our ability to avoid the implications of our empirical descriptions is amazing. For example, one text speaks of shifts and functions to the federal level, shortly after citing the Tenth Amendment as reserving powers to the states. Another states that "in theory" federalism means that each level of government is "legally supreme in its own area of jurisdiction," but the book also has a realistic chapter in which the basic assertion is that "over the years, the meaning of federalism has changed." [13] Why then don't we change the theory too? Similarly, another text speaks of each level "possessing substantial powers and independence" yet later says that "cooperation and adjustment of responsibilities are the day-to-day characteristics of modern federalism." The framers' idea, this book states, was that each level would be "supreme in its own jurisdiction"; why then do the authors never explicitly state that the framers' idea is dead, when they detail the changes from that kind of independence very carefully for some fifteen pages? [14] One of the most popular of all American government texts, that of Burns and Peltason, stated in a recent edition that "the formal structure of our federal system is little changed," but that "the way we actually operate this system, however, is drastically different." [15] If the latter, then what meaning has the former statement? It seems clear from these examples— and they could be multiplied easily by reference to additional texts—that federalism needs to be re-examined, not from the viewpoint of abstract conceptualization, but by close description and analysis of the major forms of continuing actual interaction between the national, state, and local levels of government in the United States. The empirical examination is necessary not only because conceptualization doesn't go far enough, but because we really don't know, apparently, what the actual story is. While the textbooks all state that federalism and the national-state distribution of power are vital aspects of the American polity, they differ strikingly when it comes to their images of what that distribution is at the present time and what has happened to it historically.

One text speaks of "the overall shift in power from the states to the national government," while another asserts that the "states retain prodigious powers." The latter text cites certain areas of exclusive state action;

The decision whether or not to have capital punishment; to punish murder; to monopolize the sale of liquor or outlaw its sale entirely; to permit divorce for a fancied frown or forbid it for mayhem; and to spell out how delegates to the national party conventions are to be selected or leave this to the political parties concerned. A complainer about dwindling state powers who has a more active imagination might list what states *could* claim to do if they wished: adopting the Mosaic Law as the official legal system; insisting that automobiles be driven on the left side of the street; refusing to let persons vote until they reach the age of 80; or selecting their legislators by flipping coins.[16]

Another text has a couple of pages in its chapter on federalism with the heading, "The Tide of Centralization," in which it is contended that "it is probably true that in the 1960s the trend toward federal assumption of new responsibilities is more marked than ever before in our history." [17] Using the areas of urban problems, commercial regulation, and civil rights, the authors point to the weaknesses of the states as the reason the states have "lost functions to the federal government or have been subjected to federal controls." [17] However, when speaking of such fields as health, education, social welfare, and housing, the increase in federal government activities does not represent a shift of function in the sense of taking things away from the states; rather it means a new sharing of functions the states previously took care of alone. This may be less a matter of centralization in federal hands than the creation of semi-permanent tensions and a fluctuating pattern in the distribution of power as the two levels of government simultaneously cooperate and contend with one another for policy control and administration in these jointly operated areas. While some textbooks emphasize the growth in numbers of state civil servants and the size of state budgets as an index of

18

continued state strength, others point out that despite increases in state and local activities, "the national government has grown relatively larger and more powerful." [18] On the other hand, one of the basic texts that evidences greater than normal familiarity with intergovernmental relations concludes that "there is no evidence that the expansion of federal domestic activity is depriving the states and communities of their policy-making powers. Indications are that it is not." [19] The authors of that book interestingly emphasize that the factor of professionalization common to the various levels of government tends to provide a basis for participatory leverage in policy making on the part of state and local officials because they share background and professional values with the policy makers at the national level. While these questions of the realities of the nation-state relationship are the really important ones, one cannot leave the formal aspects of federalism without at least recalling briefly the legal history of federalist doctrines down the years. The Supreme Court's views have provided at least a set of boundaries within which political forces had to contend.

The Court's Views

Under Chief Justice John Marshall, the Supreme Court stressed national supremacy and implied powers, and totally ignored the Tenth Amendment as an independent curb on the powers granted to the national government. The Marshallian precedents are largely the ones operative again today, but in between came a century in which the dominant doctrine of the Court was what the late judicial scholar Edward S. Corwin termed "dual federalism." In this conception, the distribution of powers between the two levels was seen as fixed and immutable; the states were seen as on an equal level with the national government; and the Tenth Amendment was viewed as carving out an area of exclusive jurisdiction which the supremacy clause could not touch.[20]

Interpretation of the commerce clause was central to explicating the practical meaning of dual federalism, particularly toward the end of the nineteenth century. In one sense the Court gave great weight to the commerce clause, asserting that it pre-empted economic regulation from the jursdiction of the states, so that they could not act regarding matters in interstate commerce. At the same time, the Court narrowly defined commerce (so as to exclude manufacturing) and asserted that the commerce clause stopped where the Tenth Amendment began. Thus *neither* level of government could act to regulate such matters as wages and hours and child labor. The high (or low) point of this interpretation came in 1918 in *Hammer vs Dagenhart*.[21]

In this case, Justice Day's opinion for the majority amended the Tenth Amendment by asserting that to the states "and to the people the powers not *expressly* delegated to the national government are reserved." The word expressly is *not* in the Amendment, and its inclusion by Day directly contradicts the "necessary and proper clause." The tenor of the Court at that time is inadvertently revealed in the dire fears expressed if the Congress were allowed to regulate child labor:

> If Congress can thus regulate matters intrusted to local authority by prohibition of the movement of commodities in interstate commerce, all freedom of commerce will be at an end, and the power of the states over local matters may be eliminated, and thus our system of government be practically destroyed.

This is the kind of thinking that dominated the Supreme Court until the constitutional revolution of 1937. Since that time, there has been a return to the Marshallian-Hamiltonian principle that where the national government may act at all—and that is almost everywhere under the broad interpretation of implied powers—the so-called reserved powers of the states are no impediment at all to national action. The Tenth Amendment, as noted earlier, is now seen as stating but a truism, that "all is retained which has not been surrendered." The supremacy clause is back in fashion, and the Court most definitely does not treat the states as co-equal sovereigns with the national government. In practical terms, perhaps the strongest indications of what the current interpretation of federalism permits may be seen in such legislation as the Civil Rights Act of 1965, under which federal voting registrars supplanted state officials in several southern states, and in the Supreme Court's decisions in *Baker* vs. *Carr* and its sequels, under which the one man–one vote ethic is slowly revolutionizing the composition of state legislatures.

Since the demise of dual federalism, the shorthand phrase for characterizing the existing phase of nation-state relations has been "cooperative federalism." As the words indicate, the national and state governments work together in the same areas, sharing functions and therefore power. While the Federal Bureau of Investigation has its own special roles, it also runs a training academy for state and local police officers. U.S. Forest Service personnel cooperate with state foresters. U.S. Public Health Officers work closely with the state health officers on such matters as communicable diseases or the investigation of water pollution problems, and so on. The general welfare is a matter of *joint* concern these days, with the states actually increasing their own activities at the same time that the federal presence is also growing more noticeable, particularly in financing state activities through grants-in-aid and in selecting particular problems for national priority—e.g. education, health research, the reduction of poverty.

The essential, but often overlooked, fact about today's cooperative federalism is that it revolves around cooperation in running programs—in doing things—rather than merely in passing statutes. The very nature of modern government is activist and goal-oriented. That is to say, the cutting edge of legislation today does not lie in laws simply prohibiting anti-social behavior by individuals or protecting individual rights. Instead, it consists of statutes that inaugurate administrative programs to advance definite social goals: the elimination of poverty, the beautification of highways, the provision of recreational facilities, the improvement of urban education, the encouragement of scientific research, the provision of public housing for the poor, the revitalization of the cities, the elimination of air and water pollution, the prevention of crime and delinquency, the achievement of equal opportunity for minorities, etc., etc.

Such objectives are not obtained by legislative fiat; only (if at all) by continuous programs of social action. For a variety of reasons, effective programs are most often those cooperatively shared between the national and state levels of government. Thus the currency of the phrase "intergovernmental relations" (even more than cooperative federalism), for the stress today is not on the legal, constitutional positions of the levels of government, but on their practical working relationships. Americans want problems solved. The funds for attacking problems, and often the most effective political impetus, come increasingly from the federal government. But Americans also do not want a "federal octopus"; they do not want local management of programs to be in the hands of federal officials, whether operating locally or—far worse—making particular local decisions from faraway Washington. Hence the compromise of shared functions, permitting both national stimulation and financing and state and local operation of programs to take necessary variations in application into account.

Federalism: An Attitude?

During the administration of President Lyndon B. Johnson yet another shorthand phrase came into usage: *creative federalism*. This phrase goes beyond cooperative federalism in emphasizing direct federal-city relationships that bypass the states, and—even more significantly—contractual relationships between federal agency and *non-governmental* organizations. Community action groups under the war on poverty, containing representatives of the beneficiary groups, exemplify one branch of contractual creative federalism, while the use of private corporations such as Litton Industries and Federal Electric Corporation to run Job Corps centers, or Westinghouse Corporation to devise machinery for programmed instruction, are examples of the so-called *private federalism* strand.

As long ago as 1954, Don K. Price used the phrase "federalism by contract" to describe the way in which four-fifths of the federal government's research and developments funds are used to purchase the performance of research by non-federal organizations. While the shift in constitutional doctrine from dual to cooperative federalism made possible the entry of the national government into a number of areas from which it had previously been excluded under narrow interpretations of the Constitution, the shift to creative federalism does not (at least not in all ways) represent a further centralization. Rather, it constitutes the epitome of decentralization, in the sense that the federal government not only does not hire its own civil servants to run the programs that the national legislature is funding, but it even reaches

23

below the states to local governments, to semi-public organizations, and to private business firms to administer "its" programs. Furthermore, it is not entirely a matter of administrative decentralization; it is also very substantially a question of policy making decentralization. The exact extent to which grants-in-aid and creative federalism constitute means by which policy making is shared between national and state-local levels will be examined later. Suffice for the moment to say that it has gone far enough so that one author has written a very provocative book around the thesis that the federal government has in effect lost control of its programs through excessive decentralization of policy making.[22] At this point, one might well ask whether there is anything at all left of the formal, constitutional position of the states in American federalism. The answer is that yes, there is a set of guarantees to the states, which provides that the national governments shall:

1. Guarantee to the states a republican form of government;
2. protect them against invasion and domestic violence;
3. not change a state's boundaries without its consent; and
4. maintain equal representation in the Senate for each state.[23]

The existence of the states is therefore guaranteed. Since the theory of a unitary state holds that even the existence of subordinate units is at the will of the central government (as is the case with cities within an American state), this guarantee may be said to constitute the *formal* essence of federalism. Note that this does not imply any particular relationship or division of powers and functions between the states and the national government. It is therefore largely irrelevant to the political controversies over the federal balance, for these concern the *actual* degree of centralization and decentralization and policy making powers, and the *actual* degree of independence or sharing of functions.

On this basis, it can be seen that the legal-juridical approach to federalism is rather inadequate for getting at the really important questions. Just as political freedoms depend far more on the existence of social pluralism and an ideology favorable to them than on formal constitutional guarantees—which can be effective only as a rallying point when these other conditions exist, so also with federalism. The juridical arrangement takes its meaning from and has its vitality or viability determined by sociological heterogeniety of a society. As William S. Livingston has written,

. . . the essense of federalism lies not in the institutional or constitutional structure but in the society itself. Federal government is the device by which the federal qualities of the society are articulated and protected. The essential nature of federalism is to be sought for . . . in the forces—economic, social, political, cultural—that have made the outward forms of federalism necessary. Federalism, like most institutional forms, is a solution of or an attempt to solve a certain kind of problem of political organization.[24]

This is a fruitful way of looking at federalism. It is an approach that can usefully be employed in addressing the question of the extent of decentralization of policy making required for effective and rational problem solving in a country like the United States, for where diversities are important decentralization is important, and where the culture has been nationalized then the program decisions and choices of goals can reasonably be nationalized.

Another non-juridical approach to federalism that we will find it useful to keep in mind is the relationship of the political party structure to issues of centralization and decentralization in policy making. There may be a chicken-and-egg

25

question here: Does the constitutional pattern of federalism, under which the states play an important role in the national electoral system, produce the loose, fragmented, decentralized political parties of the United States, or does the American party system produce and sustain the decentralized pattern of policy making that we call federalism? While the two are not mutually exclusive and may indeed be mutually enforcing, David B. Truman has effectively argued a case that federalism leads to a decentralized party structure, whereas the late Morton Grodzins most effectively made the case that governmental decentralization is a function of political party looseness.[25]

The essence of federalism seems to lie in the intangibles. Vile may have defined the crux of the subject when he wrote that "federalism is perhaps as much a state of mind as anything else." He continues:

> Americans have a "federal attitude" towards government which colours their whole approach to governmental problems, which insures that the solutions found to these problems will be within a particular pattern. This attitude is . . . vague and meandering, and contains contradictory elements. It is a way of thinking which enables considerable changes to take place within a broad stream of tradition, changes necessary in order to adapt to new conditions, changes which can be brought about by compromises, the elements of which are easy to find in the rich and varied ideas of American history.[26]

It is indeed an attitude, a habit of mind that leads Americans to place such tremendous emphasis upon the existence of instruments of decentralization in their governmental system. As a pragmatic people, however, Americans also want to get things done. Sometimes this comes into conflict with the notion of reliance upon state and local action. Further, our notions of what is appropriately a subject matter for local action and what for national concern changes over time. Our age does not see constitutionally fixed distributions of power and functions as the most effective instrumentality for ensuring a simultaneous maximization of effective government and decentralized government. Federalism, like the separation of powers and the institution of judicial review, was a great social invention in 1789. As with the other two basic concepts of the American scheme of government, its meaning in our day must be greatly modified from the original expectation. While we continue to be a federal system in that both levels of government continue to exist, and not on sufferance from each other, Vile's characterization of the central feature of the system as being interdependence places the emphasis exactly 180 degrees away from the position of states' righters and the conventional ideology. Whether Grodzins is right that the marble cake conception has always been in fact the dominant practice of the American system, or whether it is more accurate to say that there has been a very considerable shift in this century from a heritage of separation of functions by levels of government toward shared functions, is a question of historical fact that I am not personally able to settle, although the latter view seems to me to have the better of the argument. The crucial fact is that the functions *are* shared today, whatever may have been the story in the past. And from this flow some further questions:

In the system of shared functions, what is the balance of power? What are the sources of leverage that each level of government has over the other? To what extent does federal sharing in functions formerly performed entirely by other levels of government constitute policy making centralization? To what extent, on the other hand, can federal participation through the provision of funds for state and local op-

27

erations be seen as merely a fiscal relationship without political power consequences? These questions are closely related to, and cannot be answered apart from, a consideration of the system of grants-in-aid that is at present the primary mode by which the sharing of functions takes place, and an evaluation of the revenue sharing alternative espoused by both President Nixon and a number of prominent liberals. But that consideration has itself a necessary antecedent: a look at the over-all pattern of fiscal federalism.

II

The Policy Issues

2

The Crisis of Fiscal Federalism

One of the most succinct and graphic statements of the problem of fiscal federalism has been made by the former Chairman of the Council of Economic Advisers, Professor Walter W. Heller of the University of Minnesota. In arguing for a broad-gauged plan of sharing federal revenues with the states on a no-strings-attached basis a few years ago, Heller said that the basic reason why this is necessary is that "prosperity gives the national government the affluence and the local governments the effluents." [1] This reference to the "hot" problem of environmental pollution symbolizes the fact that in the United States domestic public services are almost all delivered to the public by state and local government units rather than directly by the national government. Social security and veterans' benefits and farmers' subsidies are provided by the national government directly, but the great bulk of public services in the areas of health, education, welfare, housing, highway construction, police protection, parks and recreation, conservation practices, and agricultural extension is provided by state and local units, although all of these (in widely varying degrees) are partially financed by the federal government today. As Heller has expressed it:

A very large part of what we do through government is done through state and local units. They are the ones to whom we usually turn as we seek to maintain and upgrade our educational efforts, improve our physical and mental health, redevelop decaying urban areas, build safer and better highways, overcome air and water pollution, and equip our suburbs with water systems, sewers, roads, parks, schools, and the like. This list is striking partly because each item on it represents either an essential function or a reasonable aspiration of a great and growing society; partly because each item falls squarely within the traditional sphere of state-local operations; and partly because so many items on the list are suffused with a national interest that transcends state and local lines and demands Federal action and support.[2]

That the areas just mentioned are ones in which we expect state and local governments to provide the services is clear. However, it is not so clear that the quality of services rendered is adequate to our needs or desires. In contrasting the prosperity of our private sector with the relative poverty of our public sector, Professor John Kenneth Galbraith (in his usual quotable manner) by implication expresses a very low estimate of that quality:

The family which takes its mauve and cerise, air-conditioned, power-steered, and power-braked automobile out for a tour passes through cities that are badly paved, made hideous by litter, blighted buildings, billboards, and posts for wires that should long since have been put underground. They pass on into a countryside that has been rendered largely invisible by commercial art. . . . They picnic on exquisitely packaged food from a portable icebox by a polluted stream and go on to spend the night at a park which is a menace to public health and morals. Just before dozing off on an air mattress, beneath a nylon tent, amid the stench of decaying refuse, they may reflect vaguely on the curious unevenness of their blessings. Is this, indeed, the American genius? [3]

Unsatisfactory though the trip may be, one can understand the city family's attempt to escape to the countryside: Riots. Garbage collection strikes. Overloaded telephone circuits. Rat-infested housing. Reading rates up, but libraries forced to close evenings and weekends. Schools that don't educate. Schools that could educate much better if they had funds. Campers outstripping campgrounds. Hospitals overpriced yet understaffed. California's conservative Republican governor cuts medical aid for the poor, and New York's liberal Republican governor begins to sound like a hard-hatter (is that related to a Mad Hatter?) as he excoriates the poor for moving into his jurisdiction and demanding public assistance without a year's residency. Without major new federal aid on the order of $10 billion, Rockefeller said early in 1971, we face a "major breakdown" in the cities. Did he overstate the case? Maybe slightly, maybe prematurely— but not by much. In its financial dimensions, American federalism is clearly a system in crisis.

The Fiscal Crisis

Let us look at the components of that crisis, and at the significant trends in governmental finance that both underlie the problem and reflect our thus-far inadequate efforts to deal with it.

The quintessential fact is that alluded to in the quotation that began this chapter: affluence lies with the national government, while the effluents are the responsibility of the

33

states and cities. In less colorful language, the proposition is that we suffer from a fiscal mismatch. That is to say, it is relatively much easier for the national government to increase its tax revenues each year than for state-local governments to do so. Yet the burden of increased demand (and expenses) for public services rests primarily at the doors of the lower jurisdictions. The result is that state-local ability to meet public demands goes down, while their dependence on federal funds and their indebtedness both increase, despite substantial revenue increases through courageous tax enactments. Let's spell out these points with some figures that show both trends over time and in the present picture.

Item: State-local general revenues, excluding federal aid funds, rose from $15.6 billion in 1948 to $95.4 billion in 1969.

Item: State-local debt rose from $24 billion to $133.5 billion in the period 1950–69, accounting for a fair share of that revenue increase. In percentage terms, that's a whopping 550 per cent jump, while the *national* debt did not even double, rising from $257 to $354 billion.

Item: The states have been having an even harder time than the localities in paying their expenses out of tax revenues. In the 1950–69 period, state debt rose eight times over, to $39.5 billion, while the local increase was about five times over, to $93.99 billion.

Item: Public school teachers constitute 40 per cent of all public employment (about half of all public employment in internal functions)—and almost all of them are paid by local government units. No wonder the local property tax is the most hard-pressed source of public revenues!

Item: Grants-in-aid, the major kind of federal funds given to the state and local governments, from $1.8 billion in 1948 to an estimate for fiscal 1972 (i.e. the year ended June 30, 1972) of $30.3 billion.[4]

34

Item: These federal grants accounted for 20.2 per cent of state-local revenue in 1969.

Item: With the help of federal grants and borrowed money, state-local government expenditures rose from $20 billion in 1949 to $121 billion in fiscal 1969. In the same period, the federal expenditure increase was from $41.3 billion to $191.9 billion, a sufficiently lower rate of increase to make one wonder why there is so much loose talk about the federal "takeover."

These figures capture the consequences of our fiscal structure. That structure itself can be helpfully looked at in two parts, the expenditure pattern and the revenue-raising pattern.

On the spending side, one finds that the most expensive domestic functions are, for the most part, the responsibility of the lower levels of government. In terms of direct expenditure (i.e. regardless of which level of government raised the money being spent), taking fiscal 1968 as an example, two-thirds of highway expenditures were made by state governments, one-third by local governments; direct expenditures on education were: federal, $2.45 billion; state, $10.95 billion; local, $30.20 billion. Of an all-government expenditure of $11.24 billion on public welfare, states accounted for over $5 billion, localities for almost $5 billion. On prisons, only $65 million was spent directly by Washington, compared with $1.27 billion spent by the state-local levels. What domestic functions, if any, are the *direct* responsibility of the national government? One is natural resources, to a two-thirds extent; others include the postal service and space research, both 100 per cent federal; and water transport and air terminals, about three-fourths federal.

If one includes indirect expenditure (e.g. federal grants to a state to use in building hospitals, the direct expenditure showing up only as a state item), the picture changes signif-

35

icantly for certain functions. About a third of highway and health and hospital expenditures are then seen as federal, and now more than half of public assistance payments. Education, perhaps ideologically the stronghold of local expenditure–local control sentiment, is more federal than expected: one-eighth of state-local expenditures are comprised of federal grant funds, in addition to the substantial direct expenditure mentioned above.

What about the other side of the coin—the tax pattern?

In a recent book Congressman Henry S. Reuss (Dem., Wisc.) argued that state and local governments are not only unlikely to raise sufficient revenue in the next decade to meet their needs, but that for them to do so would be "economically dangerous, socially undesirable, and politically improbable, since state-local taxes, as opposed to federal, tend to be inequitable and inflexible." [5] Those are strong phrases, but justified. As we shall see, state-local taxes suffer from triple disabilities: (1) they are inflexible; (2) they are regressive; (3) they are incapable of providing equal services in all states because of unequal resources on which they are based. Conversely, federal taxes are much superior, exactly because they are flexible (i.e. responsive to changes in national income), progressive (at least mildly), and provide the only effective means of achieving equalization of services among rich and poor states and cities.

The first step is to sketch the major features of the existing tax structure.

There are three major categories of taxes, and each is the primary source of revenue for a different level of government:

1. Income taxes—primary source for the federal government, equaling 83 per cent of federal tax revenues in 1968;
2. Consumer taxes (especially the general sales tax)—

primary source for the states, equaling 64 per cent of state tax revenues in 1968; and

3. Property taxes—primary source for local governments (nearly exclusive source for school districts), equaling 87 per cent of their fiscal 1968 tax revenues.

Just as each level of government is dominated by a single tax, each type of tax is largely accounted for by one level of government. Thus, Washington collected 91 per cent of all income taxes (again using 1968), while local governments collected 97 per cent of all property taxes. The picture with consumption taxes is somewhat different: although the states account for a majority percentage—53 per cent—the federal share is far from negligible at 41 per cent. However, of the general sales tax alone, the states' share was 88 per cent. It is the specific consumption taxes—on gasoline, liquor, and tobacco—that give the federal government a large consumption tax proportion.

What does it all add up to? Collectively, income taxes (in 1968) accounted for 57 per cent of all public tax revenues, consumption taxes for 22.5 per cent, and property levies for 16 per cent. Since the national government took the lion's share of the largest revenue producer, it is no surprise to find that it dominates the public revenues picture generally, accounting for 62 per cent of all public revenues in 1968, with the states at 26 and local governments at a mere 12 per cent. (Since local governments spend about 42 per cent of all direct domestic public expenditures, on the other hand, it is immediately clear that they could not function by reliance upon their own revenue sources; the significance of state and federal grants to localities is manifest.)

It adds up to something else, too: that there has been a drastic centralization in American fiscal federalism, for in 1902 the federal share was not 62 but 38 per cent; the state share, not 26 but 11 per cent; and the local share was not 12 but 51 per cent! As measured by revenues, there should be no question of the states' having atrophied, but a very considerable question of relative financial atrophy at the local level.

Not least among the reasons for federal dominance of the revenue picture is the superior *elasticity* of the income tax, which gives it a considerable political advantage growing out of an economic fact. Let's explain that a little.

Tax elasticity refers to the revenue responsiveness of a tax to changing economic conditions. A tax with low elasticity produces less than a proportionate increase in revenue as taxable incomes rise. L. L. Ecker-Racz, in his excellent brief volume on state-local finance,[6] uses the example of the cigarette tax, the yield of which rises only 40 per cent as fast as incomes. That is, a 10 per cent income increase for a state will produce only a 4 per cent cigarette tax revenue increase. State income taxes, on the other hand, have a very high elasticity: a 10 per cent increase in economic activity will yield a 15 to 18 per cent rise in revenue. At the federal level, the income tax yield runs slightly lower, but is still decidedly elastic. Property taxes have an elasticity of 1.0 (i.e. the yield is proportionate to economic growth), while the general sales tax's elasticity is probably slightly lower than 1.0, since higher income people save more and spend less (proportionately to income) than lower income families.

Tax elasticity is an economic fact. Its political implication is that the more a jurisdiction relies on income taxes, with their high elasticity, the larger the revenue increase it can obtain *without having to legislate any increase in tax rates*. The federal government's tax take goes up by six or seven billion annually, with merely average growth in Gross National Product (GNP). Yet the most noticeable change in federal tax structure in recent years was the 1964 income tax *reduction*. The political appeal of increased reliance upon federal funds as an answer to state-local fiscal needs is therefore considerable. Members of city councils and state legislatures are extremely sensitive to the electoral consequences of voting new or increased taxes, yet also to public demands for improved and increased services. Because of the latter, they have (often courageously) bitten the bullet often in recent years—but not often enough or hard enough to prevent a worsening of the state-local balance sheet. The desirable way (perhaps the only way) out of the dilemma, so far as they are concerned, is to pass the financial buck to national Congressmen and Senators, who have a much pleasanter task than their elected counterparts at the lower levels: because of automatically increasing federal revenues, thanks to tax elasticity, they need only vote to *spend* the taxpayers' funds in support of state-local services (through grants-in-aid or revenue sharing); they need not bite the tax bullet. (This suggests, of course, a self-help route open to courageous state legislatures: if all of them would enact progressive income taxes—only 39 states had done so by 1971—they would soon reap similar benefits for themselves. But they fear to take the plunge, or to increase rates sufficiently to make the tax maximally effective.)

Another major reason for a trend toward greater reliance upon federal revenues to serve the purposes of the entire governmental structure lies in the comparative *regressivity* of state-local taxes. A tax is regressive when it falls proportionately harder on lower income than on higher income taxpayers. Although the federal government uses consumption taxes—e.g. on liquor and gasoline—and these are regressive no matter who imposes them, the total impact of federal taxation is progressive because of the predominant reliance upon the progressive income tax. Congressman Henry Reuss has pointed out, in favoring use of federal revenues to support state-local services, that while the federal structure as a whole (prior to recent income tax modifications) took 18 per cent of the income of families with incomes below $2000 (showing a need for reform there, too), but 31 per cent from families with incomes over $10,000, state-local taxes take only 4 per cent from the latter families, but 17 per cent from those in the $4 to 5000 income bracket.[7] The property tax, in particular, is deservedly under attack. Partly this is because it is simply being overworked. It has increased fivefold in the last generation and accounts for half again as large a percentage of all tax revenues now as it did twenty-five years ago.[8] But also—and people seem to realize this, at least intuitively—real property is a very poor index of ability to pay and no longer is closely related to the kinds of services it is used to provide. Its anachronistic qualities are pointed up in Ecker-Racz's comments:

[In the nineteenth century] when the states granted local school districts the power to tax property, they in fact provided all children with an approximately equal educational opportunity because property value consisted largely of agricultural land and tended to be distributed in proportion to population. Property was then a good prey for people's taxpaying ability, and a tax on property could be levied and collected locally without much difficulty. . . . However, local government no longer limits itself to activities which relate to and benefit property. A large share, typically more than half of local government expenditure, is for services that benefit persons rather than properties. Since we now move about freely, the beneficiaries of today's education, health, or welfare expenditures financed by the property owners of one community are tomorrow likely to be the residents of another community. For this reason it is neither logical nor fair to continue to distribute the cost of education and welfare services in proportion to the assessed value of property to which people happen to hold title.[9]

40

The third basic characteristic of the American intergovernmental fiscal structure lies in the *inequality of resources* among the states. If the taxable capacity of the states varies widely (as it does) then the tax revenues of state and local governments will vary, too, and with them the ability of each state to meet service needs of its people. Unfortunately, with states as with families, those with greatest need for public services tend to be those with lowest resources. Although governments, too, are subject to "cost of living" differentials from one region to another, the cost savings obtainable through lower prices in rural states are not as great as the differences in tax capacity. Even by trying harder, the states with lower levels of taxable resources per capita are unable to raise as much revenue as the wealthier states.

Personal income per capita for 1968 ranged all the way from $4256 in Connecticut and $3968 in California to $2081 in Mississippi and $2790 in Utah. Taking the U.S. average of $3421 as an index figure of 100, state personal incomes ranged from 61 in Mississippi to 124 in Connecticut.[10] Even though Mississippi makes a greater proportionate effort than does Connecticut (i.e. taxing at higher rates, so as to extract a higher percentage of personal incomes), the difference in taxable resources means that the result will not be much better than half as much revenue for the state to use in supplying services to its citizens. (In point of fact, Mississippi's index of tax effort, compared with a national average of 100, is 98, while Connecticut's is 88. The range of states in terms of the tax effort index is from 139 for New York to 71 for Nevada, and 72 for Texas.) Perhaps more graphically, if Connecticut taxed its citizens' incomes 5 per cent, it would have slightly more revenue than Mississippi would if it took 10 per cent of income. The differentials indicated by comparing absolute dollar amounts spent per state on education, or public health, or public assistance for families of depen-

41

dent children are unfairly misleading about those poorer states that, like Avis, "try harder"—but without a chance in the world of becoming No. 1.

Nothing the states can do individually can overcome the differential of resources. "Bootstrapping" only goes so far. The implication is clear: If we decide as a nation that we want a certain level of education, or welfare, or health care for all persons as U.S. citizens, then only the application of the Robin Hood principle through the national government can achieve the goal. That is, by having Uncle Sam collect more revenues from the wealthier states and distribute more in grants or shared revenues to the poorer states can equalization of services be attained.

(Actually, resource disparities are at least as great between towns and counties within individual states as between states. The equalization principle therefore needs to be applied also at the level of "little federalism," by moving the financing of a larger share of essential local government services—such as education—from the local to the state level, with equalization through state grants.)

This point has received major underlining by a mid-1971 California Supreme Court decision declaring unconstitutional the prevailing pattern of primary reliance upon local property taxes for the financing of public education: the disparity of resources between school districts under this system, said the court, violated the requirement of equal protection of the laws. How the implications will be worked out (i.e. what changes in the state-local fiscal pattern will be legislated to accommodate to the court decision) was not clear at the time of writing, but it *was* clear that the decision would mean a drastic revision of public finance, with predictable reverberations across the whole country. The range of school finance within the single state of California, incidentally, is illustrated by these figures for 1969-70: the assessed valuation per average daily high school attendance varied from $205,970 in Sierra Joint Union High to $17,942 in Grant Joint Union High district, the state-wide average then being $37,445. Expenditures per average daily attendance ranged from $355 to over $3200).

At the end of his thorough review of state-local finances, Ecker-Racz concludes that "the people's prospects for sound public policies improve with the distance between voters and their elected representatives." [11] One corroboration of this sad dictum is the inability of many state and local governments to utilize fully whatever tax capacity they may have. Tax capacity is not automatically translated into tax revenues: specific legislative action is required. As often as mayors and governors have been impelled to ask for tax increases, there have been an even greater number of cases, apparently, in which they have either failed to seek increases, or have failed to obtain those sought, in proportion to expanding service needs—otherwise state-local debt would not be increasing so rapidly. Between 1957 and 1969, the per capita increase in state-local taxes ranged from 170 per cent in Delaware through 133 in California down to 100 in Connecticut and 86 per cent in Montana.[12] As indicated above, the tax effort among the states varies considerably.

"Fiscal capacity" is a political as well as an economic concept. Interstate (and intercommunity) rivalries for business location act as a severe dampener of tax-raising proclivities—where such exist at all. Although there is considerable evidence that tax factors are not particularly salient to wealthy individuals or to business firms in locating themselves, it is widely believed (or at least a fear that no one wants to test) that taxes are decisive in locational decisions. Ecker-Racz effectively sums up both sides of the situation:

> Business appears to locate its plants with an eye to the availability of labor, materials, transportation, and space, the

accessibility to markets and to other business firms with which frequent contacts are required, and a host of other variables. Increasingly location decisions by business are importantly influenced also by the quality of government services provided to business itself and to the families of the employees. . . .

[On the other hand,] policymakers in state legislatures and city halls yearn for trade and industry and tend to credit the repeated assertions of their business constituents that taxes are influential in business decisions.[13]

So long as this constraining belief exists, no conceivable changes in state-local public finance are likely to solve the intergovernmental revenue problem—even where the resources do exist.

To be fair to state-local elected officials, finally, one should note that despite interstate rivalry and the perennial fear on the part of politicians that advocacy of higher taxes is a sure route to dis-election, there have been some valiant tax actions. In the 18-month period of January 1965 to June 1966, Walter Heller reported the following "brisk business in new and used taxes":

Five states enacted new sales tax, . . . while eight others increased their rates. Eight increased their corporate income tax rates. Oregon, long a hold-out, adopted a cigarette tax, while fifteen others increased rates. Finally, seven states increased liquor tax rates and ten, gasoline tax rates.[14]

More recently, 33 increases in state gasoline taxes have been legislated in the past five years, and 54 increases have been made in cigarette taxes, with the maximum rate (in 1971) being 18 cents per pack in Pennsylvania.[15]

Shared Functions, Shared Expenditures

In the preceding section, we looked mostly at the federal-state-local mix in raising revenues. Now let's look more closely at the spending side. But first, a caveat: most statistics on governmental expenditure are of direct expenses, i.e. those from a government to its suppliers or its program clientele, and do not reflect intergovernmental transfers of funds, i.e. those granted by a higher level to a lower level to aid in the financing of a service. In such statistics, federal grants do not show up as part of Washington's expenditures, but only as part of state or local direct expenditure. Given the magnitude of grants today (from state to local as well as federal to state levels), this considerably distorts the picture in the direction of minimizing the federal role. We will try to correct for this at appropriate points. On the other hand, the direct expenditure figures are a valid measure to the extent that the significant question may be: Which level supplies the services and meets the citizen? rather than: Which level raised the money?

With these qualifications in mind, here are the facts. In total direct expenditures (including national defense and international relations), we find that over a 60-year period (but in spurts caused by the Great Depression and World War II) the local and federal shares have just about been reversed, with the states playing a smaller in-between role both earlier and now. With national defense running at $70 to 80 billion annually, and thus constituting by far the largest direct expenditure of the national government, and one of the few functions in which other levels of government do not share significantly, it is not surprising that Washington's share of total public expenditure grew so greatly. Table 1,[16] following, shows the stages of change:

TABLE 1

PERCENTAGE SHARES OF TOTAL DIRECT PUBLIC EXPENDITURE

	1902	1927	1948	1954	1967	1969
Federal	34	31	62	67	57	54
State	8	12	13	11	16	13
Local	58	57	25	22	27	33

If we switch focus to direct domestic functions expenditures, we get a better picture of the three levels of government in the truly comparable area of consumer activities. Then, as Table 2 illustrates, we find a postwar increase in the federal share, with a steadying trend most recently; an extraordinarily constant state share, and a local decline that has now leveled off, or may be in process of reversal.

TABLE 2

PERCENTAGE SHARES OF DOMESTIC DIRECT EXPENDITURES

	1902	1927	1948	1954	1962	1967	1969
Federal	17	15	23	26	27	34	32
State	10	15	26	24	24	24	25
Local	73	70	51	50	49	42	43

Considering the absolute increase in local government from $45 to 67 billion between 1962 and 1967, the relative decrease of the past twenty years becomes almost startling. Note also that the state level stability of proportion does not mean stagnation, but a very steady and substantial growth in actual dollars. With school costs accounting for not far from half the local government total, we can see that modern government increasingly passes by the local level, with more and more of domestic functions being handled by the state and national levels. (Incidentally—or not just incidentally, as a matter of fact—we say *by* the state and national levels, instead of *at* to emphasize that most of the national government's activities take place at regional and local offices around the nation. See the U.S. Government listing in your local telephone directory for confirmation that *national* does not necessarily mean *centrally* or *remotely handled*.)

The dimensions of the shift toward a more state-oriented and nationally oriented pattern of intergovernmental fiscal relations are in fact even greater than Table 2 indicates. This becomes apparent, first, if we plug in the intergovernmental expenditures and show grants-in-aid as expenditures of the *grant-giving* level. Then the picture (for non-defense expenditures in fiscal 1968) changes to an almost equal-sided triangle, so to speak. Federal expenditures are then 35.3 per cent of the all-government total; state, 31.3; and local, 33.4 per cent.[17]

The relative roles of the national and state levels may be seen in even more dramatic terms, however, if we carry this perspective one step farther, subtracting from state and local levels the amount of their expenditures financed not by their own resources but out of revenue originating as grants from above, then the shares are (1969):

Federal	43 per cent
State	29 per cent
Local	28 per cent

These figures, of activities financed by each level of government, prove conclusively that Uncle Sam is the financial senior partner of the American federal system today, quite apart from his exclusive role in external affairs.

Implications

Not unexpectedly, the constitutional and political changes that have occurred since the beginning of the century in the doctrines of American federalism have had fiscal consequences. The sharing of functions that constitutes cooperative federalism and creative federalism is seen in the cooperative financing of governmental functions. The entry of state and federal governments into operations once thought to be "merely local" is paralleled by the greater share in the financing of government operations accounted for now by these higher levels of government. Because federal grants-in-aid (the primary form of intergovernmental expenditure) have risen so rapidly in just the past few years (from $2.3 billion in 1950 to $23.9 billion in 1970 and $30.2 billion in 1971, by estimate), statistics that exclude this kind of expenditure present (as we have just seen) a very incomplete and inadequate picture of the dramatically enlarged role of Washington in the financial aspects of federalism. The fiscally subordinate status of a local government is perhaps made even more sharply evident when we recall the revenue-shares picture presented earlier in this chapter: for 1968, the federal government collected 62 per cent of all public revenues, the states 26 per cent, and the local governments 12 per cent.

In the previous chapter, Kenneth Wheare was quoted as saying that the maintenance of federalism required that regional governments as well as the central government have sufficient economic resources to support themselves, if they are to be truly independent and coordinate rather than subordinate. The brief examination of fiscal federalism contained in this chapter has demonstrated that the state-local governments are by no means financially independent. Furthermore, it seems beyond cavil that this financial dependence will increase further over time. In fiscal 1971 more than one-fifth of state-local revenues derived from federal aid. Just ten years earlier that figure was 12 per cent. If Wheare's requirements are accurate, then the fiscal facts we have just reviewed suggest that federalism in the United States is dead.

On the other hand, this position assumes what in fact needs to be questioned: whether *financial* dependence necessarily means *programmatic* dependence. William H. Young was quoted in chapter one as asserting that

. . . the States are today, for those programs involving national financing, largely administrative subdivisions of the national government . . . more susceptible to national control than ever before in our history.

That may be a somewhat extreme statement, but if we emphasize that Young has said *susceptible* to national control rather than necessarily actually controlled, then it is a statement with which many observers would surely agree. Perhaps, however, we should examine rather than assume the conclusion often jumped to, that financial dependence equals programmatic dependence.

What the development of the present-day pattern of fiscal federalism does for certain is to raise particular questions for us. We do not yet know the full implications of the pattern and we will not know it until we have explored such questions as the following:

How does fiscal federalism relate to political federalism? Does financial contribution equal political power? If fiscal relationships do matter to federalism, which is the significant aspect—how much money is supplied by each level, or, which level spends it in contact with the citizens? (The federal government is clearly dominant on the first aspect, local governments and state-local governments together are clearly dominant with regard to the second aspect. Which matters more?) The answers to such questions cannot be determined deductively. They require examination of *how* the funds granted by a higher level to a lower level of government are given; i.e. with what strings attached, or with what purposeful insulation from control. This requires an examination of the existing grant-in-aid system, its origins, operations, and evaluation, and of alternative schemes now under active discussion.

The next question might be called "the Wilbur Mills question" because it is one raised very strongly by that Congressman, who is Chairman of the House Committee on Ways and Means, in justifying his opposition to the concept of general revenue sharing. The question is: How important is the tax-expenditure linkage? That is, has the level of government that raises the money a right (or an obligation) to decide the purposes upon which it is to be spent? If one level raises the money, but allows a lower level to decide how to spend it, what are the implications for the distribution of power assumed by the concept of federalism? Although the federal government might become in time the source of more than half of state and local revenue, which would clearly make the United States a unitary rather than a federal system in its governmental finance, is it possible that this could be in fact quite consistent with continuance of a federal pattern in substantive *policy* development? That is, could there be autonomy of state and local governments in making policy decisions regarding the purposes for which they will spend their revenues—if the federal government were to turn over those funds with no strings attached?—which is the meaning of the concept of general revenue sharing that is discussed below? The existing pattern of fiscal federalism, we can clearly state at this point, is one in which the raising of public revenue is increasingly and overwhelmingly a function of the national government; it is one in which the direct expenditures—the visible connection between the government and its suppliers, clients, and beneficiaries—are still largely in the hands of state and local governments, although with the intermediate level gradually becoming larger; and it is one in which, finally, the very rapid increase of federal financial aid to the lower levels has been for purposes defined by the national Congress.

Although there are qualifications to be made on the latter statement (as we shall see in the next chapter), the role of Washington in determining or at least influencing what state and local governments choose to emphasize in their programs is clearly much larger under the existing system of specific grants-in-aid than it would be under a program of no-strings-attached revenue sharing. That is to say, the existing pattern of fiscal federalism is one that emphasizes the national political majority's sense of our substantive policy needs rather than the definition of needs that might be made by state or local political majorities. For concrete illustration, take the case of CRLA, the California Rural Legal Assistance program funded under the Office of Economic Opportunity. In July of 1971 the Director of OEO in Washington announced continued approval of the CRLA and continuance of its grant-in-aid funds for another year. This came after the Governor of California had attempted to veto the CRLA program; and he had probably done so with the approval of most of the political majority that had returned him to office in 1970.

The balance of state and national power and state and national policy-making authority that constitutes the essence of federalism is composed of numerous and complex elements. The instruments of change in that balance are also diverse. They include the political party system, whose decentralized pattern is often cited as both cause and effect of constitutional federalism, as well as Supreme Court decisions that impose national standards of behavior (presumably although not always actually in accord with national political majority sentiments) upon sometimes reluctant state political majorities—as most obviously in the case of civil rights. They also include the institutions and processes by which public funds are both raised and spent in pursuit of the goals of government. What we know at this point is that the over-all financial picture is one of great and urgent difficulty on the part of state and local governments and relative ease on the part of the national government. The national government, we also know, is already responding strongly to these needs, and has been doing so for a decade. Whether this will be enough, or soon enough, is presently being questioned, however.

What we do not know, and what much of the remainder of this book will attempt to explore, are the relative contributions to solution of our domestic problems to be made by further development of essentially the existing pattern of rather specific grants-in-aid, compared with the virtues of the widely discussed proposals for general revenue sharing which have been picked up by a Republican President after earlier espousal by economists identified with the liberal wing of the Democratic party. In addition to the comparative merits of these approaches to fiscal federalism as ways of solving problems, we shall also be concerned with their respective implications for the continuance of federalism. We might have to face the possibility that what is best for the continuance of federalism is least adequate for the solving of major problems. We might have to make a choice. It is to illuminate the choices that lie before us that these pages are written. While the author's own value position is that the present system is good, although in need of modification, and the trend toward greater national influence upon local decisions is also good, every effort is made to present a balanced and objective description and analysis of the factors involved in choice. Then the reader is helped to make up his own mind, regardless of whether he agrees or not with the author's prescriptive statements.

3

Grants-in-Aid: The Cutting Edge of Intergovernmental Relations

The best proof that the states' rights model of federalism (as a system of government in which the central and regional levels are separate and distinct from one another, each operating in its own exclusive sphere) is dead lies in the grant-in-aid system, which uses a fiscal relationship as a basis for policy making and programmatic cooperation. This system constitutes the complete embodiment of Grodzins's conception of federalism—although it remains to be seen whether the Grodzins corollary of decentralized policy making is also validated, since the sharing of functions does not necessarily mean the absence of a dominant policy making role by one of the partners to the sharing. As we describe major features of the grant-in-aid system let's keep in mind as an over-all orienting question the degree to which federal fiscal sharing in programs operated directly by state and local governments produces federal influence or power. It will quickly become clear that the answer does not lie in the sphere of quick and easy generalization; rather, it is in the area of "it depends"—on the type of grant, on the type of substantive program, on the interest group and political

54

configurations surrounding each program, and so forth. It is probably safe to agree, however, with William H. Young's assertion that "the most powerful engine in this century for reshaping national-state relations has been the 'grant-in-aid' system of national financing of state and local activities." [1] Grants-in-aid may be defined as money payments furnished by a higher to a lower level of government to be used for specified purposes and subject to conditions spelled out in law or administrative regulation. Grants are thus distinguished from, although first cousins to, the concept of general revenue sharing, which means money given by one level of government to another *without* advance specification of purpose and without specified conditions—that is, "no strings attached" aid. The range of functions in which federal-state-local cooperation takes place by means of grants-in-aid includes cooperative state agricultural experiment stations (the granddaddy of the system, started in 1887), vocational education, aid to the blind and to families with dependent children, airport construction, urban renewal, water-treatment works construction, defense-related educational activities, mass transportation, air pollution control, highway beautification, waste-disposal facilities, model cities, adult work training, and even educational television. Health, highways, welfare, education, and community development are the major categories of aided functions, with public assistance programs (more commonly known as "welfare") accounting for by far the largest single block of funds, $7.5 billion in fiscal 1970. The precise number of grant programs currently in operation depends a bit upon one's definition. Using the criterion of separate authorizations, the Advisory Commission on Intergovernmental Relations estimates a total of 530 grant-in-aid programs in 1970. Four-fifths of these were enacted after 1960; indeed 143 were instituted in the first two years of the Nixon Administration. [2]

This astonishing rate of proliferation of grant-in-aid programs is more than matched by the exploding rate of increase in the dollar volume of appropriations accounted for by the grants. The 1971 estimate was of $30.297 billion, compared with an actual 1970 figure, just one year earlier, of $23.955 billion, and a 1961 figure of a mere $7 billion. In fiscal 1947, right after the Second World War, grants-in-aid amounted to $1.668 billion, and in 1951 the figure was $2.287 billion. Making all due allowance for the impact of inflation upon these actual dollar figures, it is clear that the Congress has recently become very fond of the grant-in-aid idea. This is, as we have seen, partly in response to the state-local fiscal crisis and the consequent simple need for revenue; but it is also (and perhaps in larger part) a response to pressures from federal agencies, functional specialists in and out of government, and specific interest groups, all of whom have become well aware of the potentials of the strategy under which one obtains action in all states by using the leverage one has at one pressure point—that is, the national Congress.

The historical origins of the grant-in-aid system actually antedate the Constitution. The Land Ordinance of 1785 provided that lot number 16 of each township carved out of federal lands should be reserved for maintenance of public schools. Although most of the early grants were in the form of land rather than cash, there were a few of the latter kind. In 1808, there was a Congressional appropriation of $200,-000 to assist the development of state militia; and the early 1800s also saw cash aid for railroads and canals, supplementing the very large land grants given to the railroads. By 1915, the dollar volume of cash grants had only reached $5 million. The major categories were agricultural extension, highways, and (after 1917) vocational education. From World War I until the New Deal these programs amounted to about $100 million annually. During the New Deal there was a spurt in grant programs with the new federal aid being associated with social security programs of public assistance and unemployment agencies, aid for state and local planning and, in 1937, the first public housing program, under which the federal government provided long-term loans for state and local housing authorities to construct low rent housing and grants for slum clearance.°

The programs of the 1930s were the first to require substantial federal supervision and the first to impose management conditions upon the grants. Perhaps the most notable conditions were those for financial audits and, under the Social Security system, provision that state and local personnel participating be selected and administered under a merit system of personnel administration. Most of the programs in the early years had fairly stiff matching requirements, i.e. the receiving unit of government had to put up a dollar of its own money for each dollar it received in the form of a federal grant. In the 1960s, however, the great majority of programs were enacted with much more than 50 per cent federal participation, often 100 per cent under project grants whose major purpose was to stimulate innovation. As of 1967, about 150 of the grant programs provided 100 per cent national financing and about 90 of them 50 per cent or less.

Grants-in-aid constitute a major social innovation of our time, and are the proto-typical, although not the statistically dominant (they now constitute over 25 per cent of domestic federal outlays), form of federal domestic involvement. Although grants serve a number of different purposes, and although there are several aspects of the political and economic rationale underlying them, I suspect that the most

° For an excellent descriptive history of the development of grants-in-aid, see W. Brooks Graves, *Intergovernmental Relations in the United States* (New York: Scribners, 1964), chapters XIV-XVI.

important single reason for their popularity among both politicians and professionals of the functional areas aided is
that the grant device bypasses all the difficult questions of
governmental structure in a federal division of authority. In
this respect, grants constitute a halfway house very similar
to the post-Keynesian system of economic stabilization and
business regulation in which the public sector has a decisive
influence upon private economic activity but does so
through indirect means that avoid the structural question of
capitalism versus socialism. By using grants, one doesn't
have to face the question: At which level of government
does this function belong? If the activity is traditionally a
local one, its direct operation can remain there, while its financial problems are solved with federal aid. If the federal
government wants to inject its sense of values and priorities
into the shaping of a program, the grant provides a vehicle
for programmatic leverage without its being necessary to
take over the whole function and remove it from local
hands.

In the case of federal contracts for research and development, which have in the past twenty years made many
major private aerospace and electronics firms virtual
branches of government while remaining technically under
private ownership, the grant system permits the national
government to expand vastly its role in domestic general
welfare matters without triggering public outcrys that
would surely have considerably dampened this growth if it
had meant direct national assumption of programs, with federal civil servants taking over from state and local officials
in area after area. When one looks at statistics on public
employment and finds a rather small growth in the federal
civil service as compared with the state and local figures,
the citizen is reassured that the federal octopus has been
held in bounds. If he stopped to think about it, however, he

would realize that it's not all that restricted a role, for countless thousands of state and local officials are *de facto* on the federal payroll. That is, they constitute a "hidden bureaucracy," with salaries derived from federal grants. One might make a very rough calculation along these lines: almost one-fourth of state-local revenues come from federal grants; state-local employment was about ten million persons in 1970; therefore, one-fourth of this, or 2.5 millions, should really be added to the federal employment total—doubling it—if one were trying to draw up a total picture of the federal government's involvement in domestic affairs. In short, by whatever measure one uses, grants-in-aid are indeed what William Young calls them, "a powerful engine" for reshaping American federalism.

Types of Grants

There are several different ways that we can characterize the subdivisions of the grant-in-aid system. One important division is between categorical grants and block grants. While there is—as always with such analytic distinctions— a gray area of overlap, categorical grants are by and large those for specifically and narrowly defined purposes, leaving very little discretionary room on the part of a recipient government as to how it uses the grant, while block grants are broader in scope and although tied to a clearly stated area (such as health, or elementary education, or community facilities development) they do not specify the exact objects of permitted expenditure and hence create much larger zones of discretion on the part of the receiving government or agency. Another way of putting this is that categorical grants have a much greater potential impact on federalism —changing the locus of policy-making more sharply from the state-local to the national level—than do block grants.

In terms of federalism, state-local discretion in the use of federally provided funds is the functional equivalent of fiscal autonomy.

Beyond block grants, there is a further step in the direction of state-local autonomy in the form of revenue sharing, which is generally defined as a kind of fiscal federalism that constitutes an alternative to grants-in-aid rather than a subtype of grant. President Nixon's 1971 plans for special revenue sharing (described later in this book) come very close to what is usually meant by the phrase "block grants"; the phrase "revenue sharing," in that context, constitutes nothing but a rhetorical device to make state-local discretion *appear* to be larger than it is in fact. His plans for general revenue sharing do constitute a real alternative, as that kind of revenue sharing (at least as presented to the Congress originally) would be without any programmatic strings.

An example of the specificity of categorical grants is provided by the different programs for sewage-treatment facilities. Under one program administered by the Farmers' Home Administration, cities of less than 5500 population can apply for grants to finance sewage-collection systems. For cities with a larger population, collection systems are financed by the Department of Housing and Urban Development. In the case of interceptor sewers, which transmit the sewage from the collection systems to the treatment plants, financing is available from the Environmental Protection Agency (EPA). EPA will also finance sewage-treatment plants and sewer outfalls under the same grant programs as the interceptors, but these need not be financed under the same grant. The Economic Development Agency also plays a role in financing sewage systems; for economically depressed areas, it will guarantee loans or make grants for any segment of a sewage system from collection to outfall sewer. Normally these grants or loans will finance the local contribution required by EPA, HUD, or FHA grants. Another good example is provided in the area of recreation. A city that wants to buy open land for park purposes, build a swimming pool on it and operate an activity center for senior citizens, put in trees and shrubberies, and purchase sports equipment must make as many different grant applications as there are items mentioned in this sentence.[3] In the process of accommodating to the burgeoning demands for federal aid in the 1960s, some things got a bit out of hand. The ACIR reports, for example, that the Office of Education in HEW at one point listed eight separate programs under six different laws authorizing grants to libraries.[4]

As we shall see, what has come to be called (perhaps too cutely) "hardening of the categories" constitutes one major reason for widespread interest in the revenue sharing alternative. A more likely response to over-categorization is a probable expansion of block grants. These are not now widely used, although politicians as diverse as Senator Edmund Muskie and President Richard M. Nixon are both pushing for grant consolidation which would move in this direction. The leading example of a block grant at the present time is the Partnership in Health Act of 1966, which pulled together a number of grants previously administered separately to aid states in the treatment of several diseases. On the premise that effective administration of cooperative federal-state health programs required "strengthening the leadership and capacities of state health agencies," Congress gave them more room for maneuvering—more responsibility to set their own priorities—by consolidating into a single program previously quite separate grants in the areas of tuberculosis control, heart disease research and control, cancer, radiological facilities, venereal disease abatement, neu-

61

rology and sensory disease abatements, community health services, home health care, dental disease, chronic disease, general public health, and mental disease.

In lesser degree, the Model Cities program (under which a city can get a grant for a comprehensive attack on all the problems of a single neighborhood, as a demonstration—it is hoped—of what integrated massive efforts could accomplish) could be said to partake of the characteristics of a block program. At least, it has encouraged communities to think through a "package" of grant proposals that will all mesh together into an integrated community development program. The carrot to encourage this integrated planning is a promise that, although the grant proposals must still be acted upon individually, those which are tied to an integrated plan will receive higher priority than those which are simply *ad hoc*. However, Model Cities programs, since they must still be approved in all their components by the federal officials, do not really possess the discretion characteristic of a block grant.

President Nixon's "special revenue sharing" plans vary considerably in the degree of discretion that they would provide to the recipient agencies, although the Administration distinguishes them from block grants by eliminating matching fund requirements and maintenance of effort requirements. (This means that federal funds will do *less* than previously to increase aggregate effort, becoming more a way to enable the receiving governments to avoid raising their own money while maintaining current levels of service.) Like block grants, special revenue sharing would be allocated to identified functions in particular amounts fixed by formula. The receiving units therefore do not have discretion over use of the funds as regards the proportion spent on each of the six specified areas: law enforcement, manpower training, urban development, transportation, rural development, and education. The formulas themselves contain rather clear federal value choices, e.g. the urban development shares would be weighted toward degree of overcrowding, condition of a city's housing units, and proportion of poverty-level families. For example, the education grants are weighted toward low-income areas. Further, the states are not trusted to pass on a reasonable share to their constituent communities: urban development funds would go directly to cities; a partial "pass through" is required of transportation and education funds. What these demonstrate on the whole is that, despite the President's expressed desire to turn power back to state and local governments, political reality argues against his doing so without retaining a definite rein in Washington's hands.

Just as the grant system as a whole stands somewhere between total state-local autonomy and total federal takeover of specific functions, so also does the block grant constitute (at least potentially) a reasonable compromise between the values of categorical grants and shared revenues. Federal *policy* is very clearly stated in the laws authorizing the block grant programs, and if there is adequate means for ensuring programmatic accountability of the recipient governments, then such grants may be a useful way of centralizing policy while decentralizing administration and permitting considerable local choice and decision making on particular programs.

A second basis for distinguishing among types of grants is found in the criteria for distribution. Formula grants are to be distinguished from project grants by this means. As the name implies, the formula grant is one whose funds are divided among all eligible recipients on the basis of some announced criterion that is applied proportionately across the board and without any discretion in the hands of the grant-giving officials. An example is provided by public-assistance grants for aid to the blind. Under this program, the national government promises to match state payments of benefits to blind persons in accord with a statutory ratio. The needy blind in every state are eligible and the national government is committed to supplying its share of the benefits for as many persons as the state welfare departments certify as eligible. Formula grants are distributed to all eligible jurisdictions as a matter of "right." The discretion, if there is any, lies in the hands of the recipient governments that decide how much matching money they want to use to obtain a particular federal grant. Federal influence under formula grants lies in the administrative requirements that accompany the grant, rather than in the substance of the grant.

In project grants, on the other hand, which require specific approval by federal agency officials of the proposal made by a potential recipient government or agency, the potential for federal influence and control is decidedly greater. Project grants are made to meet specific problems and are not spread among all potential recipients according to any fixed proportions. Although every community in the country may be eligible for a waste-treatment plant grant, for example, the funds available for the program will sharply limit the number of communities that can be aided. In such a situation, the community whose proposal most nearly satisfies the definitions of appropriate action in the minds of the federal officials administering the grant program will be the successful one. As President Nixon said in one of his revenue sharing messages, "Because competition between localities for limited Federal dollars is most intense, local officials are highly motivated to meet both the formal requirements and the informal preferences of Federal officials as they file their applications." [5] Urban renewal was one of the earliest and remains one of the most significant of project grant programs. A community wishing to avail itself of this aid for slum clearance is required to draw up a workable program, that is, in federal terminology, to engage in sufficient planning to persuade the Urban Renewal Administration that in drawing up its specific request, it has carefully assessed its community needs and potential, whether this be for low-rent apartments or clearing land for a new downtown commercial center to increase the tax base, or whatever.

On the other hand, with about 430 of the 530 grant-in-aid programs being of the project type, there is considerable room for state-local discretion in "shopping around" to decide which grants to put their energy into applying for. Indeed, because a certain amount of both energy and administrative sophistication is required to do an effective job of preparing proposals, it may be that the project grant often does not go where the financial need is greatest. As of 1970, half of all federal grant funds were in project grant form; this proportion has been rising steadily since the mid-'fifties.

Both the advantages and the problems of project grants are well illustrated by the history of the community mental-health centers. A *New York Times* story of June 29, 1970, contained the statement that "it is federal policy to promote local initiatives." (That's an interesting paradox in itself— that local initiatives now require a national government stimulus!) The particular initiative referred to was the development of community mental-health centers, under a program inaugurated by the National Institute of Mental Health. This federal grant program was too successful: it encouraged the creation of more mental health centers than the federal government said it could afford to support, even though they had all been begun in anticipation of federal aid for staffing. In fiscal 1970, some 123 new grant requests were made and approved by the Institute, but the agency then found that its funds would permit funding of only sixty-three of these projects. As of a year later, twenty-seven of the carryover applications had been funded. With new applications coming in, the fiscal year ended June 30, 1971, seeing 55 staffing grant applications recommended for approval but left stranded without funds. Perhaps twenty of these found other sources of funds, and so became operational for some services.[6]

Purposes of Grants

Decisions regarding when to use formula grants and when to use project grants, and evaluation of the merits of each type, depend partly on the purposes for which one has a grant at all. We sometimes assume off-hand that the purpose of all federal grants-in-aid is financial in nature: to supplement inadequate state-local resources. This is too simple. At least as important as the purely financial objective are the following:

1. To establish minimum national standards in some program that exists in all states, but at widely differing levels. The outstanding current example of a movement in this direction is the Nixon-Mills Family Assistance Plan, the plan which fundamentally revises the public assistance system to establish an income floor of $2400 for a family of four. This is in contrast to the previous program of aid to dependent children, for example, under which monthly payments per child on so-called welfare ranged from $8 to $88, depending upon which state one resided in.

2. Equalization of resources. Closely related to the first objective, the emphasis here is upon the use of the federal tax system to apply the Robin Hood principle: to take more money from the states with higher per capita incomes and transfer it to those with lower per capita incomes, enabling the latter to upgrade their public services. Many federal for-

mula grant programs have sliding scales that vary federal contributions from one-third to two-thirds, inversely related to the capacity of receiving states to raise their own funds.

3. To improve the substantive adequacy of state programs. Under project programs particularly, in the process of inviting, aiding in the design of, reviewing, and approving proposals from state-local agencies, officials of the grant-giving agency have an opportunity to provide technical assistance in accord with the highest professional standards. Inasmuch as only a few states are able to compete with the national government in attracting outstanding professional talent, such technical assistance can be an important vehicle for upgrading the quality of public services at the state level. Graves evaluated the standard-setting impact of the Hill-Burton Program for planning and constructing hospitals with federal aid with these summary comments:

> The introduction of a continuing state-wide planning program is a landmark in the field of hospital and medical facility planning and construction, while the utilization of standards of adequacy and the development of patterns for distributing facilities within a State has resulted in important gains in hospital planning and better distribution of health facilities. Another important accomplishment of the program has been the development for the first time of minimum standards of design, construction and equipment for hospitals and other types of medical health facilities.[7]

4. A related way in which the federal government may improve state programs, concentrate a "critical mass" of attention in a given area, and avoid useless state duplication and the frittering away of energies in many efforts no one of which can be adequate, is exemplified in air pollution research grants from the National Air Pollution Control Administration. If California, New York, Idaho, and other

states with air pollution problems were to go their independent ways on their research, there would be a great deal of waste of money, in addition to which no one of them could afford to spend enough to do an adequate job. Federal grants can be the catalyst for bringing a unified research program into being out of the cooperative efforts of all interested states.

5. The stimulation of experimentation, and the demonstration of new approaches, are major objectives of a high proportion of the project grant programs in the areas of health care, education, human resources development, and community development. The National Defense Education Act (NDEA) of 1958, for example, responding to Sputnik I, gave specific federal grants to enable schools and colleges at all levels to obtain equipment and generally beef up their instructional programs in the teaching of science, mathematics, and foreign languages—areas in which we were embarrassed suddenly to find ourselves lagging behind the Russians—supposedly. Sometimes the stimulus is not for a program that is in itself innovative, but simply to get more communities to do something quite ordinary but which they don't get around to on their own. The sewage-treatment plant program inaugurated in the late 1950s is a good example of this. The number of treatment plants under construction jumped several-fold in the first three years of operation of this grant program. Apparently, federal money stimulated the cupidity of local governments, if nothing else, making it hard for them not to do something for which the federal government would pay half the cost.

Perhaps the most experimental and stimulative—too much so for many politicians involved—of all federal grant programs were the community action programs under the Office of Economic Opportunity in its early years. OEO grants, begun in 1964, were used to stimulate substantive experimentation in treating the symptoms and causes of poverty in more free-wheeling ways than the traditional social welfare agency pattern had permitted. Project Head Start, which has been even more successful politically than educationally, is perhaps the outstanding illustration of programmatic experimentation. Under Head Start, as many readers will be aware, disadvantaged children of preschool age were given a kind of enriched nursery school experience in the hope that this would compensate for their non-middle class home background and put them on a par with their more advantaged classmates when they reached the first grade. Although there is apparently much evidence that the gains attributable to Head Start are lost unless the intensive effort is carried forward within the school as well as before school, the program did have a sufficient impact so that it has been institutionalized as a regular part of the federal government's contribution to the educational process.

Another novel service to the poor, that of class action law suits on behalf of the victims of finance companies and installment merchandisers, has also won sufficient attention and has sufficiently proven its worth so that President Nixon has proposed separate institutionalization for its concept. Even more stimulative of experiment than the substantive programs undertaken by OEO was the unheard-of process of encouraging the poor to participate in the design and implementation of their own programs and encouraging them to organize politically to work their way into American politics, or, as the late E. E. Schattschneider put it, to work their way into the pressure system from which the poor have traditionally been excluded.[8] It is safe to say in the case of OEO grants that the experimentation in clientele policy making generated by the innocuous-sounding phrase "maximum feasible participation" ended up being a good deal more experimental than nine-tenths of the government officials and legislators associated with the program ever expected or intended—or wanted. The perhaps quixotic ideal of "participatory democracy" has been at least partly realized in actual practice: through the operation of grants to community action programs, participatory democracy is more than a theory.

Let us note here an interesting point about the thesis of federalism as a system that encourages the use of the constituent units as experimental laboratories, with an opportunity for what has been experimented with successfully to be applied through the national level of federalism to other constituent units. The induced changes in political structure and in substantive policies that made the OEO grant so controversial did not take place according to the mythological formula. Instead of a few states or localities experimenting with an idea that had welled up spontaneously at the local level, these astonishing experiments came about because an agency of the central government (drawing upon some expertise developed in a foundation-sponsored program for dealing with youth problems) *mandated* a new kind and degree of citizen participation at the local level as a condition for receiving national government funds. Alliances developed between functional professionals working in the local CAPs and in OEO headquarters—alliances that constituted a kind of functional federalism as a conscious alternative to the predominantly status quo orientation of the regular government structures under the control of local elites. In short, what the OEO grant program has conclusively proven is that experimentation *can* be directed from above. Indeed, sometimes that is the only way it can be started at the local level.

6. Improvement of state-local administrative structure and operation. At least since the adoption of the public-assistance grant programs in the mid-'thirties and the 1939 amendment to the Social Security Act that established a

merit system requirement for participating state agencies, the general administrative requirements attached to a great number of federal grants in a variety of substantive areas have been extremely important in inducing grant-receiving governments to professionalize their organizational structures and their personnel and financial practices. Merit system and auditing requirements have had double effects. Directly, they have established new standards of competence and accountability in the agencies handling federal funds. Indirectly, these standards have constituted, if only by contrast, bench marks against which to measure the quality of operation of state agencies not subject to federal supervision. While a few states have always been the equal (even occasionally the superior) of the national government with regard to administrative quality, the great majority has been extremely laggard in adopting modern management knowledge. The national government has therefore played an indispensable role in relaying to the states the management knowledge it has itself developed and assimilated from the most advanced private business practice. From the standpoint of maintaining a healthy federalism, the administrative improvement impact of the federal grant system upon the states may have been at least as important (i.e. by improving state-local government capacity to govern) as the provision of funds.

7. Encouragement of general social objectives. The "boiler-plate" provisions of federal programs (i.e. the provisions that are automatically included in every grant agreement between the grantor agency and the grantee government) have also been used as inducements to attain unrelated social objectives. The most notable among these is, of course, the non-discrimination clause that has made grants-in-aid a potent lever in the struggle to persuade the more recalcitrant state governments to provide public services equitably to their minority populations.

8. Minimize the apparent federal role. Perhaps the most important political achievement of the grant system is to have solved the apparent dilemma arising from the American electorate's contradictory desires (a) to attack problems that the state and local governments lacked the resources to handle while (b) not enlarging the federal government. The solution to the dilemma is that the federal role is in fact enlarged, always in financial terms and often in programmatic terms, without that enlargement being apparent either in the size of the federal civil service or in the number of occasions upon which the individual citizen deals with a national functionary. It is a nice way of having one's cake while eating it. Recent Presidents of the United States have prided themselves on reducing the size of the federal bureaucracy, or at least in reducing its rate of growth to very minimal proportions. They have also prided themselves on the increasing help they have given to the solution of domestic problems through new and enlarged grant programs. They have never, however, put the two together so as to acknowledge that the first claim could be made only because a result of the second claim was to increase greatly the size of the bureaucracy at the state-local levels (as mentioned earlier). Of course, we shouldn't push this too far. It is certainly still true that direct federal operation of the funds and programs represented by the nearly $30 billion of current federal grants-in-aid would considerably further increase the federal "presence." Not all of these purposes apply to all grants, or even to any individual grant. Yet each of these purposes is significant for a number of grants.

Rationalizing the Grant System

Closely related to, yet conceptually distinguishable from the functions served by a particular grant program are the economic and political rationales underlying the entire grant system. If one sees grants-in-aid as occurring largely in areas once thought to be the more or less exclusive provinces of state-local governments under a federalized "division of labor," then the question becomes, What justification is there for the national government to enter the picture, even through grants-in-aid, let alone through direct action programs? From an economic standpoint, there are two parts to the answer. First, the simple fact elaborated earlier, that it is much easier to raise the needed revenue for public service operations at the national level than at the local level, although the problems for which the revenue is needed still have to be handled at the local level. Second, and this is an argument much developed in recent years, there stands the doctrine of external or "spillover" benefits. This says that when an expenditure produces benefits that are felt beyond (i.e. spillover) the jurisdiction of the governmental unit making the expenditure, it is proper that all benefiting jurisdictions share in the cost. Otherwise, some of them are engaged in free-loading.[9]

Education provides a handy example. Education provides tangible financial benefits both to the individuals educated and to the taxing jurisdictions in which they reside. The reason for this is simple: the more education a person has, on the average, the greater will be his earning; the greater his earnings, the greater the material satisfactions he can provide for himself and the larger the amount of taxes he will pay. Less tangibly, but perhaps more importantly in the long run, an educated populace is an essential precondition to effective democracy. If, then, the per pupil expenditure on education in California or New York is much higher than the national average of the states, every time a person educated in one of those two states moves to a state with a smaller per capita education expenditure, the latter state receives external benefits that it has not paid for. In a nation with the mobility rate that ours has (20 per cent of the population moves each year), and given the fact that school system expenditures vary as much between communities in any one state as they do among states (because of heavy reliance upon property taxes whose yield varies greatly from one location to another), the external benefits attributable to public education expenditures extend to the entire nation. At another level, that of graduate education in the universities, the spillover aspect is even more notable. A National Science Board report recommending increased federal aid says that:

> Graduate institutions are national resources. The graduate student body, especially at larger institutions and at the doctoral level, is drawn from a wide geographic area, frequently from the entire Nation, while trained scientists and engineers provided by graduate education are also highly mobile and distribute themselves nationally as career opportunities warrant.
>
> . . . The maintenance of an adequate supply of well-prepared teachers of science and engineering for service at all educational levels is a matter of national concern.[10]

According to a leading authority on intergovernmental fiscal relations, George F. Break, categorical grants-in-aid are economically justifiable only on the basis of and to the extent of their externalities or spillover benefits. He suggests that in evaluating grant-in-aid programs we ask of each program whether it generates external benefits, the exact nature of those benefits, and how important they are. By applying our scale of values regarding the importance of the projected benefits, and assuming that we can measure in some way the extent of the benefits, then we have a basis for determining the appropriate federal share of expenditure in that area. The conceptualization here is somewhat in advance of our empirical knowledge (that is, while we know what to measure, we do not yet know how to measure it in many instances), yet the reasoning is generally persuasive. Writing in the summer, and in a state that receives a very substantial influx of summer visitors, I can well see a spillover benefit from the recreational resources provided by the State of California, and therefore a good reason for national taxes to help support those recreational resources, since many non-Californians will be enjoying them.

Even in the absence of spillover benefits, however, there is a strong political rationale for federal grants. One of the more thoughtful analyses has been provided by political scientist Phillip Monypenny. In a 1960 article he argued that federal grant programs were a response to a

> . . . coalition which resorts to a mixed federal-state program because it is not strong enough in individual states to secure its program, and because it is not united enough to be able to achieve a wholly federal program against the opposition which a specific program would engender.[11]

It is a truism of the politics of policy making in the United States that some interest groups are more effective at state and local levels and others at the national level. Labor unions, for example, have their membership concentrated in about one-third of the states. Since these are the large industrial states with many Congressmen and many electoral votes for the Presidency, their weight is considerable at the national capital. At the state level, it may be considerable in ten or fifteen states, but falls off to zero or perhaps even a negative impact in many other states. Many industrial interest groups, on the other hand, find that they receive more sympathetic hearings at state capitals than in Washington.

75

Any group that wants something done at the state level, but has its greatest political clout at the national level, will naturally turn toward a grant-in-aid approach in order to combine the two.

Further, an important impetus toward grant-in-aid programs arises from the most fundamental feature of American federalism—that to achieve action at the state level means to mount a campaign in fifty different locations, while to mount at the national level requires and encourages centralized, unified action in one place, which is generally easier to achieve. Once the national government has been persuaded to enact a program, the leverage of "free money" can be counted upon to encourage many of the states to join in. Granting that ancillary political campaigns will sometimes be needed at the state level, the effort becomes a good deal more effective when preceded by national authorizing legislation. The reasons, incidentally, for not seeking a directly national program are not only the lack of sufficient political power to achieve that possible goal, but also the fact that wholly national action runs into more ideological obstacles than does federal aid, so one simply may have no desire to substitute national for state action, but simply want to beef up state action.

A final over-all reason for bringing the federal government into previously state-local problem solving through the grant-in-aid device is that the definition of what is national and what is local has changed, as well as our conception of federalism, which has gone from a competitive to a cooperative image. In terms of *Realpolitik* it has been well said that "any objective is manifestly and significantly national in character which survives the arduous, lengthy 'testing process' that Congress provides with its polycentric power structure and limited majority norms." [12] That may sound too simple or even too cynical, yet when one tries to grapple with the question of what is a national problem, or what situations warrant national action, it is difficult to find any other single criterion that will fit every instance. Only two generalizations seem to be quite certain. One is that many more problems today than in the past are national in the sense of being affected by developments elsewhere in the nation or having their own impact upon other parts of the nation. Our society has become thoroughly interdependent in its economy, its transportation and communication patterns, etc. Second, what can safely be left to local discretion is not answerable across the board; it depends on particular functions. This is true not only of relations between the national and state governments, but even of relationships between a city as a whole and its neighborhoods. Consider, for example, James L. Sundquist's comment in a discussion of the implications of decentralization under the Model Cities program:

> The extent to which the city can defer to neighborhood opinion varies by function. It may be able to accept neighborhood control on local rezoning issues, for example, while to defer it at all on the enforcement of an open housing ordinance would be to nullify the law. Each neighborhood cannot have its own freeway plan. Each cannot be the hospital center of the community. Salaries paid to employees of neighborhood organizations need to be standardized in the interests of equity. Equality of public services among neighborhoods has to be equalized.[13]

Furthermore, there seems to be hardly anything that we think of as local that does not have national aspects: consider the very local function of police protection, which today has national dimensions in the training of local police officers at the FBI academy, and in the research and development aimed at crime prevention through grants under the

77

Omnibus Crime Control and Safe Streets Act of 1968. And what could be more national than the draft that compels young men to enter the armed services in defense of the national security? Yet the draft has operated very largely through local board decisions, and the local boards had apparently very broad discretion in interpreting the criteria under which one fellow was selected and another deferred, at least during General Hershey's long tenure at the head of the system.

One of the major official efforts to lay down the conditions under which national government action was justified concerning domestic problems was represented by the Commission on Intergovernmental Relations that reported to President Eisenhower in 1955. Its *Report* specified the following conditions:

1. When only the national government has the resources for the job—e.g. defense, economic stabilization;

2. when the activity cannot be handled within the geographic-jurisdictional limits of the lesser governments —e.g. radio and television frequency allocations and regulation;

3. when national uniformity is required—e.g. the provision of currency (how broad a category might that be today);

4. when one state's action or inaction may hurt other states—e.g. hindrances to interstate commerce, resource conservation; and

5. when a state fails to protect basic political and civil rights that apply throughout the United States.[14]

Although I characterize this Commission's efforts as "major," these criteria are really useless, for they beg the difficult questions: how does one decide which activities "cannot be handled" at the lower level? How does one decide when national uniformity is required? The answer, of course, lies in empirical case-by-case examination of each problem. When such examination reveals that the problem cannot be resolved effectively at the local level, then one has a national problem.

Unemployment, for example, is clearly a national problem: there is nothing that any one city or state can do to solve a problem of cyclical unemployment in an interdependent national economy. Let's take a harder case: how about air pollution? In one sense, it is clearly local. That is to say, it could largely be solved in the Los Angeles area irrespective of what is or is not done about solving it in New York. At the same time, there are dimensions that go far beyond Los Angeles. One is the need for national action to assure that automobile manufacturers in Detroit produce the least smog-producing cars possible. Another is that the elmination of smog requires a great deal more scientific research than Los Angeles alone could afford to provide. Since the research that will aid Los Angeles in solving its smog problems would also help with the air pollution problems of Idaho and New York and Chicago and New Orleans, and since it would be senseless for each of those jurisdictions to duplicate the research performed by the others, it makes a great deal of sense for the national government to participate in the financing of that research.

Some problems are national in that they are indivisible across the nation. Unemployment, as mentioned, is one of these. Other problems are national despite divisibility because they exist nation-wide, that is, in cities throughout the country. Urban rioting may be an example. Although its manifestations are localized to given places and times, its roots appear to lie deep in the structure of our society, in aspects of our culture that are national rather than locally differentiable. Just to complicate the picture a little bit more, consider President Eisenhower's intervention in the

Little Rock school integration crisis in 1957. Federal troops were called into play in a situation of one high school's failure to comply with constitutional requirements announced by the Supreme Court. Although it was national action, it was very much pinpointed to a specific local situation. Therefore it exemplifies the proposition that the national government *can* take local circumstances into account in its actions, perhaps just as well as can a local agency.

In an important book on the problems of administering grant-in-aid programs, James L. Sundquist argues that in about 1960 the grant-in-aid system underwent a fundamental change. Prior to that date, he writes, "the typical federal assistance program did not involve an expressly stated *national* purpose. It was instituted, rather, as a means of helping state or local governments accomplish *their* objectives." Legislation passed since 1960 is characterized by "forthright declarations of national purpose, experimental and flexible approaches to the achievement of those purposes, and close federal supervision and control to ensure that the national purposes are served." [15] He suggests that aid for highways, hospitals, sewage-treatment plants, and the building of airports all constituted instances in which the federal grants really are *in aid* of state-local functions. On the other hand, in the cases of urban renewal, area redevelopment, manpower development, the poverty program, and model cities he contends that the grants are for the purpose of getting the state and local governments to participate in the administration of programs designed to achieve objectives chosen by the national government initially. Urban renewal, dating from 1949, he includes in the latter group as an early exception, incidentally.

Whether the original impetus for a grant program in a particular area came from state-local officials, or from federal officials or national legislators may be important in terms of legislative history, but does not, I think, matter much in the operation of programs once enacted. Even if it was the states that originally set the goal of "getting the farmers out of the mud," when the federal government enters the highway picture by supplementing state financing isn't it making that goal a national goal also? * Since the federal government does not aid every single state and local purpose, in the process of selecting those purposes that it will aid it is making a determination of the state-local functions in which there is the greatest national interest. As Sundquist himself later suggests, as major domestic problems develop, public attitudes pass through different phases. First, a problem is seen as local. Secondly, federal aid is proposed to help the states solve *their* problem. Finally, the problem is redefined as being national and requiring a national solution which the states merely help to bring about.

So we come back to the beginning. Those things are national and justify grant programs which the Congress *says* are national. The concepts of local and national interest are squishy at best. What matters for present purposes is that both constitutionally and politically we have as a nation accepted the notion that it is appropriate for the national community to imbed its scale of values (i.e. those values that a majority of national legislators can agree upon) in programs that offer state and local governments financial inducements to be persuaded that the national scale of values should also be the local priorities. In assessing the long-range trend line

* Minor historical footnote: Even the conservative, "states' rights" oriented Commission on Intergovernmental Relations disagreed with Sundquist's position. In its 1955 *Report* (p. 119) the Commission said that "The National Government has used the grant-in-aid primarily to achieve some National objective, not merely to help States and local governments finance their activities. Specific objectives have been as varied as getting the farmer out of the mud, assisting the needy aged, providing lunches for school children, and preventing cancer."

of federalism, this is to say that the balance is shifting toward the dominance of national majorities over state and local majorities, with cooperative action toward national objectives replacing the futile deadlock of the old competitive dual federalism.

Preliminary Balance Sheet

Although complete evaluation of the grant-in-aid system we have been describing must await further analysis and elucidation of revenue sharing as a widely heralded alternative, it is possible and desirable at this time to draw up a preliminary balance sheet of the system's accomplishments and its problems. The most obvious accomplishment of federal grants is to enable state and local governments to do much more for their citizens than they could afford to do with their own resources. To say that grant-in-aid funds account for over 20 per cent of state-local revenues is to say that those governments would do one-fifth less for their citizens without federal aid.

The political corollary of this financial advantage is, of course, to keep the states alive (if not well), forestalling what might otherwise be the total collapse of federalism through the political and financial bankruptcy of state government. Whether most state governments deserve the confidence placed in them may be a matter for debate, but that confidence has been so placed is undeniable, as William Anderson points out:

> Instead of by-passing the states and setting up its own direct services, the national government has in most cases, by proper inducements, enlisted the services of the state governments in national endeavors. If in such services the states do not decide all the major questions, they certainly do decide

many of them and are consulted about the others. Thus they retain practically all their self-government even in these federally aided fields. When the alternatives are considered, I doubt that any better ones have been proposed for achieving national objectives while preserving the self-government of the states.[16]

Anderson's enthusiasm may be slightly overdone, but I think that all observers would agree that the states are stronger because of federal grants than they would have been in the absence of grant funds and the grant system's stimulus to improved performance.

If, as the late Morton Grodzins and his disciples have argued, modern federalism is and must be cooperative rather than competitive, then one has to say that the grant-in-aid device constitutes a major social invention. It is what makes cooperative federalism a functioning reality instead of just a constitutional lawyer's phrase. Intergovernmental cooperation does exist in forms other than grant-in-aid, also. (An example would be local, state, and national police forces sharing information and techniques.) But the grant relationship is far and away the most decisive means of intergovernmental cooperation today. Because it solves (or at least ameliorates) the fiscal problem of modern federalism while permitting widely varying degrees of federal influence along with the funds, it makes the continuation of formal federalism possible.

A by-product advantage of the grant system that is not always given sufficient attention is the way in which it enables the national government to provide technical assistance to state and local governments. Since, by and large, the national government can better tap top-drawer professional talent, whether of highway engineering, social insurance, housing-market analysis, or education, than can a multitude of state and local governmental bodies, it is in a position to bring such talent to bear on local problems in a way that the jurisdiction having the problem could never afford to do autonomously. Further, even when the professional innovation takes place initially in an individual state, the existence of a national grant-in-aid program provides a means for information transfer from the initiating state to all others which would not otherwise be available. From this standpoint, one could even say that it is a good thing that the state and local governments are in a financial bind! If they could afford to act entirely on their own and the federal grant system had never been started, they would often be acting at a much lower level of professional quality than is now the case when the federal government sets the standards.

We have mentioned earlier that there is a varying structure of interest group power at different levels of government. Because of this, the grant-in-aid system also serves as a way by which the national government can respond to societal needs not politically strong in many states, stimulating states to act in areas that would otherwise be neglected because of the short-sighted, status quo views of local elites. The poverty program, aid to education, community mental health, and environmental protection are all areas that fit this description in a number of states. The more general point to be made in this connection is that the grant-in-aid system accomplishes an in-between answer to what would otherwise be a stalemate: the state-local level can't or won't solve all its problems with its own resources, yet the electorate appears not to want the entire responsibility transferred to the national level. Therefore, through grants-in-aid we find a way to put the resources where the problems are: to get the jobs done. In this connection, too, it also seems probable that the total public sector expenditure on domestic problems is augmented beyond what it would otherwise be. That is, it is politically easier to spend the money through a grant program than it would be either to spend it on a directly national program or to get equivalent amounts appropriated by the sum of the state legislatures.

Finally, there is a somewhat tangible accomplishment of the grant-in-aid system that may be more important than the financial resources the system provides. This accomplishment consists of injecting more of a public interest perspective into the operations of state-local governments than would otherwise be present in most cases. Walter Lippmann once defined the public interest as "what men would choose if they saw clearly, thought rationally, acted disinterestedly and benevolently." [17] The national government comes much closer to filling that prescription than can the state and local governments, particularly as regards fullness of resources. As with a private individual or a family, if one has barely enough money to buy food and clothing for today, one is likely to let the future take care of itself. So it is with governments: what is needed tomorrow will often be sacrificed to what makes things easier today. Similarly, what will be of general benefit to everyone, but perhaps not always of specific benefit to any one individual, tends to get pushed aside. The development of recreation areas for a growing population exemplifies both of these tendencies and problems. As George Break writes,

There is a strong possibility that states, with their continuous preoccupation with short-run financing problems, will undervalue, or even ignore, the future benefits to an ever-growing population of a widespread system of public parks and wilderness areas. From its position of greater fiscal affluence, the federal government is in a better position to judge these matters and to finance the necessary land acquisitions before it is too late.[18]

One can hardly blame the retiree on a fixed Social Security pension who takes a short-sighted view and votes against community needs in order to hold down the property tax that constitutes his primary financial burden. The federal grant-in-aid system is an essential and effective device for counteracting the short-run tendency, and thereby encouraging state and local governments to improve the quality of living for the future.

The System's Problems

Like every other human invention, the grant-in-aid system lacks perfection. Four types of problems that the system either fails to solve or self-creates need to be mentioned. First, the strong trend toward project grants, which are very useful for targeting the aid and for stimulating innovation, also has less desirable consequences. Project grants, for one thing, tend to run counter to the need for equalization of resources among jurisdictions. Those state and local governments which have the best professional staffs are likely to prepare the best proposals and thus receive the most project aid. Yet they are likely also to be the jurisdictions that are already most alert and have the best financial bases, and therefore the least need. There is perhaps an exception to this in the case of the very largest cities, which have both high degrees of professionalism and some very poverty-stricken neighborhoods. But for many other communities, there is a real question whether the project grant system may simply make the rich richer, as it were. Closely related is the fact that the awarding of funds on the basis of competitive proposals places a premium on "grantsmanship," a rapidly developing form of what is more generally known as "gamesmanship." To the extent that this is the case, relative capability in manipulating language to please federal administrators may become more important than relative objective need in determining which communities receive the most aid.

A related set of charges that are sometimes made against the entire grant-in-aid system rather than just specifically of project grants is that they tend to skew state-local budgets. The argument is that, to the extent that formula or project grants require matching funds from the receiving government, state legislatures and city councils will be coerced into putting their money where the grants are, even if those are not the areas of greatest local need. It is hard to resist a program that enables one dollar to become two or three, when the same dollar has no "multiplier" effect of this kind when used for some other area. Since grants are fairly tightly defined and do not cover all possible areas of state-local need, the inflexibility of the grants perhaps requires that receiving governments be overly flexible in accommodating to Washington's priorities.

This problem may be somewhat lessened today, as compared with ten years ago, because of the proliferation of grant authorizations. That is, there are now so many grant programs for so many different purposes that, although each is very narrow, the local government can get what it wants by picking and choosing among the programs it decides to enter.

The other side of the coin, however, is that the proliferation of programs has created a very substantial coordination problem at both the giving and receiving levels of the grant system. As the Advisory Commission on Intergovernmental Relations has said,

. . . excessive categorization and overlapping of grants create administrative problems at all levels and handicap the development of a coordinated attack on community problems . . . state and local governments may be bewildered as to the differences between seemingly like programs or uncertain

as to whether they are using the more appropriate program
. . . confusion is aggravated by the existence of varying requirements under similar programs, which may cause applicants to seek the program which seems most attractive from
the standpoint, say, of non-Federal matching required although overall considerations, such as the specific uses as to
which the money can be put, may make it less attractive.[19]

When communities are whole beings, but programs for their
development are separately categorized and separately administered by separate agencies, some classic confusions result. One such instance concerned conflict between an urban
renewal development that had been approved by one
agency for a location through which another planned a free-
way.

Finally, the grant-in-aid system can, of course, do nothing
to help the states and cities directly as regards their lack of
funds for services that lie outside the aided categories.
Moreover, to the extent that aid programs call for matching
grants, the city or state may be simply more hard-pressed to
finance its unaided services.

Primarily because of these last two problems associated
with the existing grant-in-aid system—the proliferation of
narrowly specific categories and the inability of the grant
system to solve the problem of inadequate financing for unaided services (such as fire departments)—and as a matter
of great ideological concern over the "federal octopus" in
some quarters—a great deal of enthusiasm has recently
been expressed by both liberals and conservatives for various plans by which categorical grants would be supplemented by the institution of revenue sharing between the
national government and the states. In the next chapter, we
turn to a description and evaluation of the revenue sharing
alternative.

4

Revenue Sharing — Panacea or Cop-out?

Few policy initiatives ever have had as interesting a lineage as revenue sharing. In 1958 then-Representative Melvin Laird introduced a bill in the House of Representatives. Laird (who has more recently been Secretary of Defense in the Nixon Administration) was a Republican Congressman from Wisconsin. His bill received no noticeable attention. In 1960 Professor Walter W. Heller of the University of Minnesota presented a specific version of revenue sharing which was later to become known as the "Heller plan," but his version did not at that time receive any more attention than Laird's had. From January of 1961 until June of 1964, Heller was Chairman of the Council of Economic Advisers in the Kennedy-Johnson administrations, where he was able to proselytize quietly for the revenue sharing concept. Not until almost the end of his tenure, however, was serious work done on the concept in the executive branch. When federal personal income taxes were reduced in 1964, some of the advocates of the "new economics" feared that federal budgetary surpluses would result any way, and that these surpluses would create a drag on economic activity. As political liberals, most of these economists feared equally that the existence of surpluses would inevitably produce demands for further tax cuts, although they felt that there was a great need for these additional funds to be spent in the public sector rather than to be returned to the individual taxpayer's pocket. Apparently they felt that there would be inadequate political muscle to see that the prospective surpluses were turned into federal expenditures through expansion of existing domestic general welfare programs. Revenue sharing—the Heller plan—therefore seemed an attractive alternative. One that ensured that more funds would go into the public sector, and yet avoid the objection of increased direct activities on the part of the national government.

A pre-election task force appointed by President Johnson and headed by Dr. Joseph A. Pechman produced a report late in 1964 that further developed the revenue sharing idea. Reportedly because of petulance over advance leaking of the Pechman report contents, or perhaps for other reasons, Johnson never released the report and never publicly further espoused revenue sharing. By 1967–1968, more than a hundred bills embracing over thirty variants of the revenue sharing idea were introduced in the 90th Congress. In 1965 a liberal Republican group, the Ripon Society, had adopted the concept of revenue sharing, and the bipartisan Advisory Commission on Intergovernmental Relations strongly recommended the use of revenue sharing in a 1967 report.

By the time that President Nixon was inaugurated, revenue sharing had also been endorsed by the National Conference of Governors, the National Conference of Mayors, the National Conference of State Legislative Leaders, and the National Association of Counties. As part of his call for a "new federalism," President Nixon in August of 1969 made his first major appeal for a revenue sharing program in a special message to Congress. His proposal received no hearings by the appropriate committees in the Congress, however, and it appeared to have a very low priority among Administration plans.

Nineteen hundred and seventy-one was to be a different story. The President made revenue sharing, in a vastly expanded form, a very major item in his State of the Union address, and the White House began sending special messages to Congress embodying in concrete form the President's expanded plans for both general revenue sharing and a new form of support to which he applied the term "special revenue sharing." This time there was no shortage of attention—although the most important attention was negative. Representative Wilbur Mills, Chairman of the House Ways and Means Committee, immediately announced his adamant opposition and promised to hold hearings for the purpose of killing the plan. During the spring and summer of 1971 Nixon and Mills jockeyed for political advantage, with the Arkansas legislator fairly certain to scuttle the President's program, but perhaps in the end likely to come up with a revenue sharing plan for the cities specifically. By August of 1971, the new "battle plan" for price-wage stability had pre-empted all of the President's attention to economic policy, and he deferred until 1972 the fight for revenue sharing.

Revenue sharing was thus first introduced into Congress by a Republican legislator; then advocated and developed by an economist high in the councils of two Democratic Presidents' administrations, increasingly endorsed by legislators and national associations of government officials on a non-partisan basis, and, finally, it became a major plank in the "must" legislative list of a Republican president. What is the source of this extraordinary political sex appeal? How have liberals and conservatives, states' righters and federalists come to push an identical program so enthusiastically?

What is it about revenue sharing that makes it seem the answer to all our fiscal and political woes? Finally, when it has so many things going for it, why isn't it getting anywhere?

The Case for Revenue Sharing

The economic base of the argument for revenue sharing is the same as that for other forms of federal aid: state and local governments that have to supply domestic services don't have the revenues with which to do it properly, while the federal government can anticipate steadily growing revenues without having to raise the level of taxation—and not all of that revenue growth is generally needed for the functions that the national government performs directly for its citizens. Beyond this, however, there are some differences between fiscal liberals and fiscal conservatives. The liberals see revenue sharing (like grants-in-aid) as a way of increasing public expenditures and beefing up public sector services as a taxpayer's contribution to the standard of living. Conservatives tend to see revenue sharing more as a way of substituting "stringless" federal funds for local property tax funds, rather than as a source for a net increase of expenditure.

The major financial argument for revenue sharing as differentiated from grants-in-aid is that the general operation of state and local government is as much in need of financial support as are the specific services embodied in the categories of the existing aid system. Walter Heller puts it this way

> It is hard to argue that the benefits of sanitation, green space, recreation, police and fire protection, street maintenance and lighting in one community have large spill-over

effects on other communities. Yet, in more or less humdrum
services such as these lies much of the difference between a
decent environment and a squalid one, between the snug
suburb and the grinding ghetto.[1]

In addition to the facts that grants-in-aid do not cover every
area of state-local services and are not given to cover the
general administration "overhead" of those governments, it
is argued that the matching funds requirements of many 'categorical grant programs place an unconscionable and un-
bearable strain on the poor governments. They feel they cannot afford to pass up the federal aid that is available, yet to
meet the matching fund requirements of those programs
they must strip the unaided functions of their share of locally raised revenue. It is further argued that categorical
grant-in-aid funds are too undependable, that state and
local governments cannot plan adequate programs when
these depend upon federal aid funds that may be given this
year and withheld or reduced next year, depending upon
the whims of the appropriation process in Congress. Shared
revenues, on the other hand, would be based on a permanent appropriation law that would set aside a special fund
(in President Nixon's 1971 plan, 1.3 per cent of taxable personal income) at a fixed percentage of the personal income
base, which is a much more predictable amount than are
the existing annual appropriations. Once the formula was
settled (and the Nixon formula is based on population plus
a small adjustment to reward those states which make the
greatest relative tax effort of their own), then the states
would know quite closely the amount of money they could
expect to receive year after year. Since the Nixon plan requires that the states and their cities agree on a specific percentage of the states' revenue share that would be passed
through to the cities or else accept a national government

division of about 50–50, the cities also would have dependable foreknowledge about this aspect of their revenues.

(The uncertainties of the existing system are well illustrated by the community health centers problem mentioned in Chapter 3 and by the history of so-called "impacted areas aid." This is money given on a formula basis to school districts for the number of children in the school system whose parents live on or work for a federal government installation —most often a military base—in the community. Since federal installations do not pay local taxes, the impacted areas aid is a kind of "in lieu" payment. This program, begun in 1950, is so solidly established among school systems and Congressmen that its continuance year after year would seem to be as certain as anything can be. But exactly because it is so well established, it has been used as a political football by recent Presidents, who use it to balance their budgets. The way this works is that the President announces that he is recommending termination of this program and therefore does not allocate any budget for it, thus reducing contemplated federal expenditures. At the same time, he knows perfectly well that in the end the Congress will restore that item to the budget. He thus simply hopes to shift the blame for part of federal expenditures. While sophisticated school officials know that this is the general pattern, they cannot responsibly assume that the minuet will always come out according to the script. Since school districts often are not allowed by law to engage in deficit financing, this means that they must plan their programs on the assumption of not receiving impacted areas aid and then try to expand them at the last moment if the aid does come through, or, more likely, plan to include impacted areas aid at about the same level as the previous year, and then face the possibility of having to make drastic program curtailments on very short notice if the aid does not in fact materialize.)

Although these economic reasons for revenue sharing are important, there would not be so much hoopla over changing the form of federal aid if it were not for the more significant political arguments. First and foremost among these is the assertion that the health and vitality of American federalism can be maintained (some would say restored) only if the states are given the financial resources they need along with the authority to make their own decisions regarding the allocation of these funds. The implicit assumption regarding the existing federal grant-in-aid system is clear: that it is producing (or has produced) inappropriate federal domination of state-local choices. Revenue sharing would therefore counter this trend effectively, and indeed reverse it, because it is of the nature of revenue sharing that it be given without programmatic strings. The Administration's revenue sharing plans would have as constraints on the expenditure of the funds only a pass-through requirement to ensure that the urban areas receive a fair share, and a requirement that the funds not be spent in a racially discriminatory manner. Although there are some important differences between Richard Nixon and Walter Heller with regard to their philosophies and attitudes regarding the functions of the national government (we will allude to these a little bit below), there is surprising similarity in the Pollyanna-ish quality of their flowing rhetoric on the virtues of state and local government. Let us quote Heller again:

> . . . it would be a mistake to assume that the case for federal support rests wholly, or even mainly, on . . . relentless fiscal pressures and handicaps. Far from being just a fiscal problem . . . the issue touches on the very essence of federalism, both in a political and in a socio-economic sense.

> Indeed, it is from the realm of political philosophy—the renewed interest in making state-local government a vital,

95

effective, and reasonably equal partner in a workable federalism—that much of the impetus for more generous levels and new forms of federal assistance has come.[2]

. . .

Transcending all other considerations, as we seek new forms of Federal fiscal relief for the states, is the need not simply to increase their resources but to restore their vitality; not simply to make them better "service stations" of federalism but to release their creative and innovative energies; not simply to pay lip service to "states' rights" but to give substance to local self-government.

State and local officials . . . need an opportunity to worry not just about where the next dollar is coming from but what the world is coming to. [Revenue sharing] would offer relief from the intense fiscal pressures that lead to default and dependence; would help the nation tap not only the skills and knowledge but the ingenuity of our state and local units; and would enable these units to flex their muscles and exercise greater discretion and responsibility. It would help them hold their heads high and fulfill their intended role as strong and resiliant partners in our federalism.[3]

Despite his enthusiastic hopes for a renaissance of the states and localities, Heller remains a strong exponent of a major federal domestic role. He believes that categorical grants-in-aid should remain at the heart of federal aid, and that the federal government should indeed "sharply step up its wars on poverty, ignorance, blight, disease, and pollution that beset our beleaguered cities."[4] In this respect he differs from his strange bedfellow, President Nixon, who shares Heller's enthusiasm for federalism and state-local revitalization, but who thinks, apparently, that this should be done largely at the expense of the national government's ability to set national goals at all. In his 1969 message on revenue sharing, President Nixon, apparently referring to his own election, opined that "a majority of Americans no longer support the continued extension of Federal services. The momentum for Federal expansion has passed its peak; a process of deceleration is setting in." In his view, the "problems of the cities and the countryside stubbornly resisted the solutions of Washington" during the five years or so prior to his election, with a resulting loss of popular faith in the efficacy of the national government. The proliferation of grant-in-aid programs he saw as producing "a gathering of the reins of power in Washington," which in turn he pictured as representing "a radical departure from the vision of Federal-state relations the nation's founders had in mind." He then spoke of his administration's commitment to reverse the trend of the last three decades and characterized his first revenue sharing proposal as "a turning point in Federal-state relations, the beginning of decentralization of governmental power, the restoration of a rightful balance between the state capitals and the national capital."

In his 1971 State of the Union message he put the case even more strongly, asserting that the federal government was now "so strong it grows muscle-bound," while the states and localities "approach impotence." (The latter will come as something of a surprise to federal program administrators who are acutely aware of the difficulties they face in trying to cajole state and local officials into complying with the spirit as well as the letter of federal grant authorizations. As I was writing this, the administrators of the public assistance program had recently had to threaten withdrawal of funds in order to get the states of California and Arizona to comply with statutory requirements, and a gubernatorial veto had held up the refunding of the California Rural Legal Assistance program, which was a part of the federal government's War on Poverty.) In his State of the Union message, therefore, President Nixon said, "Let us put the money where the needs are. And let us put the power to spend it where the people are." Inadvertently commenting on the panacea quality of his revenue sharing ideas, he said in his revenue sharing message to Congress of February 4, 1971, that what we need "is a program under which we can enjoy the best of both worlds." We would, he said, "combine the efficiencies of a centralized tax system with the efficiencies of decentralized expenditure." Having the best of both worlds is a child's dream that rarely comes to fulfillment in adult life. I don't believe that Nixon's revenue sharing plans are any exception, as will be argued below. In addition to the rhetorically significant yet highly intangible argument that revenue sharing is needed and would be effective in revitalizing the state-local role in American federalism, there are some more concrete reasons of a political and administrative nature.

The single greatest appeal of revenue sharing is that on the surface it appears to combine both the liberal desire for an enlarged public sector, and the conservative desire to avoid further enlargement of the federal government. (I say "on the surface," however, because—as we will argue further in a moment—when it gets down to cases the question is not just whether the public sector is extended, *but in what directions*.) Heller has said that he thinks the politically realistic alternative to revenue sharing is likely to be federal tax cuts. If that premise is correct, then even those who would like to see national direction of nationally funded programs would prefer the revenue sharing alternative, which at least provides an opportunity for more public expenditure on domestic problems, than to see these needed funds dissipated through federal tax cuts that did not of themselves produce any added revenues at the local government level. Many political conservatives would come to the

98

same conclusion from an opposite direction. They would argue that the realistic alternative to revenue sharing is not tax cuts or reduction of the national debt, but increased appropriations in the existing grant-in-aid programs. Since they see these as an instrument of the devil to maintain federal dominance, they prefer revenue sharing, which at least puts the allocation decisions at the local level where conservative, anti-public sector, pro-status groups know they have the greatest say. Thus are pairs of strange bedfellows joined.

One line of reasoning favoring revenue sharing upon which both conservatives and liberals can agree lies in a major shortcoming of the categorical grant system—the administrative cumbersomeness caused by "hardening of the categories," and by minute specifications of the categories. The recent proliferation of grants at what really is an outstanding and astonishing rate by any man's measure (from 132 aid programs in 1960 to an estimated 530 in 1970, with about 400 of these being of the project grant variety) has unquestionably created an unhealthy premium on grantsmanship. And there is also the quite understandable sense of frustration on the part of state and local officials who are trying to face real problems and whose efforts at using the federal aid that is ostensibly offered are hindered at every turn, or at least so it seems to them, by excessive restrictiveness that does not take local needs into account. As President Nixon said in his 1971 message on revenue sharing, the

> . . . system of categorical grants has grown up over the years in a piecemeal fashion, with little concern for how each new program would fit in with existing old ones. The result has been a great deal of overlap and very little coordination. A dozen or more manpower programs, for example, may exist side by side in the same urban neighborhood— each one separately funded and separately managed.

"Managerial apoplexy," as the Advisory Commission on Intergovernmental Relations has called it, is the result of these factors and of the administrative complexities that attach to very specific grant programs. Especially when the programs are of the project grant variety, rather than by formula, the applicant can be involved in reams of paperwork and engages necessarily and inevitably in a good deal of shadow-boxing or rhetorical substitutes for real compliance with federal guidelines. In fact, we are told that the guidelines for aid programs have become so complicated that in some instances there have now been published special guidelines on how to interpret the program guidelines.

The complaint about existing categorical grant programs as a reason for adding a revenue sharing system to provide no strings attached funds goes farther than this in the mind of President Nixon and other ideological opponents of central government. At this point liberals and conservatives separate again, for the liberals are not likely to have the same objections as the conservatives to the fact that, as President Nixon accurately states it, "Money is spent instead for the things Washington wants and in the way Washington orders." Allowing for qualifications on this statement, it is probably safe to make the fairly broad generalization that people like Heller approve of shared revenues in an ancillary relationship to categorical grants that do indeed give Washington an opportunity to set the priorities on the expenditure of the national taxpayers' money, while Nixon and associates seemingly regret that the entire grant-in-aid program cannot be switched over to the revenue sharing form. Were that to happen, all domestic priority setting in the fields of aided services would be set by the states, without any national say.

To anticipate briefly a point made in greater detail later on, it is possible to remove some of the unnecessary rigidities of the categorical grant system without going all the way to unrestricted revenue sharing. President Nixon's special revenue sharing plans are an in-between step of one kind, and Congress has occasionally tried other steps, most notably the creation of a few block grants. The strength of the political forces that underlie particularization of the categorical grants is demonstrated, however, by the fact that each of the block grants tried in recent years has undergone successive sets of amendments, bringing about the reduction, year by year of the breadth of discretion permitted to the receiving governments. This suggests that Wilbur Mills is more in accord with political reality than Richard Nixon; i.e., neither the voters nor the legislators are going to let the choices of how to spend federal funds be left to state-local decision-makers who are not accountable to the national taxpayer whose money is being used. That there are local variations in need and also legitimate local variations in priorities of governmental aspirations, as proponents of revenue sharing and of letting the state-local governments have a larger say in program choices are always insisting, is beyond argument. What are matters for debate, however, are: (1) exactly how much discretion to give to state-local officials and how much program goal specification to leave in the hands of the national Congress, and (2) how big a price in either corruption or simply ignorant and ineffective choices on the part of state-local officials is one willing to pay for the gain of enlarging the decision making options at the lower levels? The position being taken here will be that one should not pay much of a price at all to permit local officials to spend federal funds as they see fit. It will be argued that they have sufficient freedom of this kind with the revenue they raise themselves, and that nationally determined priorities are the proper ones to implement when federal funds are being used.

The Case Against Revenue Sharing

Let us dispose fairly quickly of some of the arguments against revenue sharing which I judge to be either untrue, or unimportant if true. Part of the opposition is of an ultra-conservative variety with which neither this writer nor most of the American electorate will agree. It is argued that the shared revenues approach is wrong exactly because it does make it easier to come up with more public money to enlarge public sector services, and that it does not require state-local legislatures to face the wrath of the taxpayers before taking more money out of their pockets. The hope is, of course, that increased taxes would not be legislated; the preference is for lessened public services as a whole, regardless of which level finances them. A long-time spokesman for fiscal conservatism, retired Professor Harley L. Lutz, for example, takes a "plague on both your houses" position, arguing against both revenue sharing and the grant-in-aid system. To Lutz's mind,

> . . . the right kind of tax sharing would be a simultaneous phasing out of Federal grants and a reduction of Federal taxes. This would be a real sharing of the Nation's pool of taxable resources, and it would reduce and eventually eliminate dependence of States and localities on Federal assistance.[5]

According to Lutz, any device by which Washington helps pay state-local government costs "is certain to be demoralizing." Only when money is "collected in the sight and with the knowledge of the taxpayers" will it be handled frugally, he argues.

Lutz also exemplifies another closely associated conservative fear, namely, that quite contrary to the assumptions of President Nixon and Walter Heller, even "no strings attached" grants will increase rather than decrease state dependence upon the federal government. "The faucet," writes Lutz, "can be turned off at will and the flow of money can be manipulated to penalize states that get too far off the federal reservation." He says further,

> When popular resistance to Federal domination rises to a pitch that will impel people to reject Federal benefits and insist that such matters as are proper governmental responsibilities be managed and financed at the State and local level, there can be decentralization of governmental power, but not before.

Here it seems to me that Lutz is absolutely correct. The leverage of Washington over the states is not just a result of specific legislative directives. Rather, it exists because of the financial need on the part of the receiving governments, regardless of the terms on which the grants are made.

In fact, it seems to me logical that revenue sharing would increase rather than decrease state-local susceptibility to federal influence. After all, in the existing form of fiscal federalism there are at least some areas—including the heart of general local government—in which federal aid programs are not a substantial factor and in which therefore local decisions really are autonomous. Under general revenue sharing with a pass-through to the cities, there would be a complete intermingling of federal and state-local revenues, such that any auditing and accountability requirements imposed by the national government would apply to the entire gamut of state-local operations. There would no longer be any area of which the governor or mayor could say, "You don't help us finance this, so stay out." When Uncle Sam aids financially in all areas, he will have a potential voice in all areas.

There is, I think, an important distinction to be made between state-local ability to make some programmatic decisions without legal requirements for review by a higher level of government, and state-local psychological dependence and susceptibility to informal federal influence because of the leverage that financial aid creates. While it is true that the federal government always hesitates—partly because of the very tradition of federalism—to impose the sanction of withholding funds upon grant-receiving jurisdictions that waste or misuse them, it is undoubtedly also true in part (whether equally or more or less, I am not certain) that state-local authorities will hesitate to insist fully upon what may be their legal perogatives when applying for a federal project grant whose approval depends upon the informal conceptions of the grant reviewing officer in a Washington bureau office. So I think Lutz is fundamentally right, that revenue sharing will not restore or maintain federalism in the sense of state-local independence of Washington. Rather, I think revenue sharing would, in the long run, put another nail in the coffin of federalism, even though in the short run it would undoubtedly permit state and local governments to make more programmatic choices on their own. Given the history of block grants alluded to just a little bit above (i.e. the tendency of Congress to start out with a broad grant of discretion and then tighten it year by year as it builds up a set of feedback responses), it seems plausible to me that general and special revenue sharing would, after there had been a number of revelations of misuse of funds, and after the states had become thoroughly dependent upon this additional federal money, turn into a device by which

Washington would say "if you want to keep getting this money, then spend it in the ways we say."

Another objection, advanced by conservatives but to which many who call themselves liberals can also subscribe, holds that to separate decisions on how to spend tax money from decisions on how to raise it is irresponsible and likely to encourage freer spending by the government that receives the politically "cost-free" revenue. Wilbur Mills, Chairman of the House Ways and Means Committee and an implacable foe of revenue sharing (at least until rumored Presidential ambitions are alleged to have encouraged him to begin to favor revenue sharing for the cities), has said that "I'm not going to be a tax collector for anyone but the federal government." In a way, this is good conservative doctrine of ancient lineage. One whole school of economists has long argued that a legislative body proposing a new public expenditure should always be required in the same measure to propose a new tax to cover the expenditure. The assumption is, of course, that under those conditions few new expenditures—and therefore few new taxes—would be authorized. If political economy were a matter of pure reason, there would be a good deal to recommend this system. Indeed, it is largely the way local government operates, because few cities have any surplus of revenue from existing taxation and therefore must raise the property tax by an amount sufficient to cover any new expenditures when setting the next year's budget. At the national level, however, it simply doesn't work that way, inasmuch as the growth-oriented income tax produces $7 billion or more of increased revenue annually without having to raise the tax rates. It is this money, at least in the first instance, that is available for revenue sharing or other expenditure. Since the voters and voters' representatives have long since approved the existing tax rates, presumably the government is already authorized to spend the resulting revenue. The fear expressed by Wilbur Mills in this connection is that revenue sharing would gradually increase as the state and local governments came to appreciate having no strings attached money which they bore no responsibility for raising. In his view, "we already have too little restraint on spending programs at the present time. If the revenue-sharing machine is to be cranked up, I fear we will lose much of what restraint we now have." [6]

To the contention by Mills and others that when one level of government spends the money raised at another level it will be spent less responsibly and with less sensitivity to taxpayer pressures, President Nixon made a reply in his revenue sharing message. His reasoning seems to make a good deal of sense. Said the President:

> . . . giving states and localities the power to spend certain Federal tax monies will increase the influence of each citizen on how those monies are used. It will make government more responsive to taxpayer pressures. It will enhance accountability.

> The reason for this is that "accountability" really depends, in the end, on accessibility—on how easily a given official can be held responsible for his spending decisions. The crucial question is not where the money comes from but whether the official who spends it can be made to answer to those who are affected by the choices he makes. Can they get their views through to him? Is the prospect of their future support a significant incentive for him? Can they remove him from office if they are unhappy with his performance?

> These questions are far more likely to receive an affirmative answer in a smaller jurisdiction than in a larger one.

The President is, I think, correct on this point. In fact, it is exactly because he is correct and because those effective local pressures will more often than not reflect status quo conservatism of the dominant local elite that liberals prefer to see the spending priority decisions made at the national level. There is an interesting paradox of political philosophy here. In the theory of representation, the Burkean notion that the legislator should vote his own conscience and his own judgment rather than simply reflect the public opinion poll sentiments of his constituency is always labeled as the conservative position. Populistic democracy, on the other hand, insists that the legislator should be merely a delegate, instructed to vote the will of his constituents rather than his own will. Yet in American politics of policy making, it is the liberals who support the notion of having priority decisions made at that level of government where the legislators are most free to be Burkean, i.e. where they are least likely to lose the next election simply because they vote in favor of one spending program that many of their constituents dislike.

Whether one is liberal or conservative, Nixon would seem to have the better of the argument over Mills so long as revenue sharing can be covered largely out of existing taxes, for to do so avoids the issue of who will decide on new taxes to support the new spending.

In one degree or another, the arguments presented so far represent broadsides against all federal financial aid and reflect an outmoded and quixotic conception of states' rights federalism. They are not very strong arguments. The better reasons for opposing revenue sharing center on its own false assumptions and on inadequacies that can best be avoided by strengthened federal expenditures and programs, the funding and operation of which can, however, be shared with state-local agencies operating under nationally established priorities.

The basic conception of revenue sharing embodies a

mythological and very false assumption derived from a half-true aphorism. The saying is that "he who pays the piper calls the tune." The truth in the saying is that he who pays the piper has a leverage for potential say regarding what tune is played, but the leverage may not be exercised, the potential may not become actual. That is why it is only a half-truth. It is the contention of Nixon and other proponents of revenue sharing that the existing categorical grant system does not leave any room for a state-local voice in program decisions. This is the basis of their assertion that there is insufficient flexibility in the system and that it cannot accommodate to variations among state and local needs and preferences. It has to be immediately conceded that there are legitimate variations of priority and preference among state and local governments and that there does need to be a reasonable amount of room for discretion. As Walter Heller has said, "the good life will not come, ready-made, from some federal assembly line. It has to be custombuilt, engaging the effort and imagination and resourcefulness of the community."

The fact of the matter is that categorical grants *do* leave room for state-local contributions to the design of programs and for state-local decisions on particular priorities within the programs once legislated. For example, take the public assistance system. While the national government puts up half the money for welfare aid, the largest category of which is Aid to Families with Dependent Children (AFDC), it has largely left the policy making decisions to the respective state legislatures. Most crucially, the level of benefits is entirely up to the states, with the national government guaranteeing to pay specified shares of the benefit level each state sets according to a legislated formula. On residency as a requirement for receiving welfare, the Congress had long set a five-year upper limit within which the states were free to do as they pleased, with some states requiring only 60 days while others required a year. While it is true that the federal government over the years has exercised a good deal of influence over state public assistance programs, as Derthick has described in detail,[7] most of that influence has been on the periphery of the program and mainly on administrative aspects such as insistence upon a merit system among civil servants handling the program and upon due process and equality in the treatment of clients. To the extent that the states act at all as social laboratories of experimentation in the classic mold (a question examined a little bit below), it has usually been a case of one or two states leading the way voluntarily and helping the national government to design a program which is then imposed from above on the rest of the states. In this way, the leading states do share in the development of federal programs. Unemployment compensation is an example in this category, as is air pollution control.

Furthermore, while it is true that many of the categorical aid programs (of a project grant variety) inaugurated in recent years have been very narrow and specific, it has been interestingly and I think persuasively argued that when there are many, many grants in a given area, the local prospective grantee agency can pick and choose among those for which it applies in such a manner as to make effective its own priority choices rather than those of the federal grantor. In this sense, one can speak of "resource mobilization" rather than "resource allocation." That is, the potential recipient government puts together the package of grants for which it applies, choosing from among 500 now available, and in this way has a very decisive say in the impact of federal grants upon itself.[8]

There is yet another dimension to the question of state-local sharing in categorical grant decision-making, and it derives from the professionalization of government today. Few indeed are the programs that really reflect simply an electoral will, a response to a "gut feeling" among the voters. Our system works much more indirectly, and the major mediators between the people and the nation's problems and the policy making officials of the government on the other hand are the professionals and the administrators in each field. That is to say, public housing is designed not directly in response to or accord with the ideas of potential occupants, but in accord with the ideas of housing experts and administrators of the Housing and Urban Development Department. Welfare amendments are generally considered only when proposed by the social worker fraternity, largely persons sharing the same outlook and professional values by having attended the same kind of graduate school to attain M.S.W. (Master of Social Work) degrees. A leading analyst of state-local government, Professor Charles R. Adrian, has argued that the major disputes over policy development tend to take place between the professional experts and administrators at each level against the politicians at the same level, rather than between the levels of government. The County Welfare Commissioner, the State Director of Welfare, and the heads of the welfare program in the Department of Health, Education and Welfare, that is to say, are all likely to have the same generally sympathetic attitude toward welfare recipients. Congressmen, state legislators, and elected county supervisors, on the other hand, are all likely to reflect the suspicious attitudes of the dominant economic elites in their election districts toward welfare.[9] One might say, in fact, that the major political disputes over the shaping of grant policy do not involve arbitrary dominance by the national government without taking into account state-local wishes, values, and experience, but revolve around the question of which state-local groups will the national government heed in designing its programs: the state-local politicos or the state-local professionals of the functional field for which policy is being made? The choice between revenue sharing and grants-in-aid cannot, therefore, properly be made on the basis of whether or not one wants to make room for some state-local sharing in the design of programs and in decisions regarding particular uses to be made of programs. Such participation can exist under either form of financial aid. The participation argument is really a red herring. (See also the paragraph below concerning whether state and local governments are "closer to the people.")

Now we can turn to what I think are the real and very major arguments against revenue sharing as even a partial substitute for grants-in-aid. The first relates to the capacities of state governments—or rather their proven incapacities. State governments are structurally inadequate and politically weak even when not actually corrupt.

Even today, one-third of the state legislatures do not even meet in regular session every year. And when they do meet, one can hardly expect their members to give primary attention to the job when they are so often paid on the assumption that this is a sideline to a career as lawyer, real estate or insurance dealer, or farmer. New Hampshire pays the members of its state legislature $100 annually. With all due respect to those New Hampshire legislators who voluntarily put forth their best efforts and concentrated attention as a "charity," what can one really expect on the average when the state is so niggardly regarding its own government? Despite a streamlining effort that has gone on for a couple of generations, too many state governments on the executive side still hamstring their governors to such an extent in an effort to keep them from doing evil that they lack sufficient authority to do good. Two years is a rather short term in which to get any major changes accomplished in today's complex world, yet that is still the term for governors in about ten states. In some states, furthermore, the governor cannot succeed himself. In almost all states we still suffer from the long ballot: we elect so many state officials who are therefore accountable only to their own constituents and not to the governor of whose administration they are presumably a part, that the governor lacks authority to run his own shop. In a vitriolic but provocative and telling article entitled "Why Bail Out the States?" Christopher Jencks argues that state governments are unlikely to attract more than a few of the most talented people. The most talented people, he points out, "are the most mobile, and in any given community the 'natural elite' is likely to be composed largely of recent arrivals. Such men usually think in national terms, taking little interest in state politics." On the other hand, there will be a few important wealthy older men in each community who do pay attention to state and local affairs, but they are not inclined to run for the state legislature. The result, says Jencks, "is that candidates for the legislature tend to be local hacks sponsored by more sophisticated and powerful men." On the executive side, Jencks says that many state governors are capable men but that they "soon discover that their state is essentially ungovernable," so they use the governorship as a launching pad for senatorial campaigns. State civil servants tend to be less than first-rate because state legislatures set salary scales too low to attract first-rate talent. Then, argues Jencks, a "vicious circle is established," in which the legislature refuses to raise salaries because the people already on the payroll seem to be incompetent. To the argument that reapportionment will cure all ills of state legislatures, Jencks has what I think is an unarguable reply:

The Mississippi Legislature would be no less a farce if it included a dozen more white supremacists from Jackson and the Gulf Coast and a dozen fewer from the Delta plantations. The Illinois Legislature will be no less corrupt when reactionaries from downstate are supplanted by a few of Mayor Daley's henchmen from Cook County. Similarly, the trouble with Massachusetts' politics is not that Boston and Newton have too few votes; it's that people like the Saltonstalls, Lodges and Kennedys do not spend their time trying to clean up the State House; they want to use their home state as a springboard to Washington.[10]

Because the states are structurally inadequate and cannot attract very much first-rate talent on the average, a political vacuum is created into which flow the lobbyists for special business interests whose strength derives more from money than from popular appeal to the electorate. That is, if government leaders are incapable of leading, private leaders are more than willing to pick up the ball and run with it. Lobbying is presumably just as heavy in Washington as at the state capitals, but there is a decisive difference: publicity, particularly that provided by a vigorous and well-financed and independent press, strengthens the national legislator's backbone and inhibits him from giving in to the lobbyists' blandishments. Furthermore, each Congressman covers a larger area than a state legislator and is more likely to have varied interests among his constituents, thus making it easier to avoid being dominated by any one interest. State governments, unfortunately, as Jencks writes,

. . . exist in something close to a publicity vacuum. Both the quantity and quality of newspaper and television coverage is inferior to that given national affairs, and the ease with which state affairs can be manipulated by special inter-

113

ests is proportionately greater. . . . The voters seldom know
who their representatives in the state capital are, much less
how they stand on various issues.

While a few states do have salary scales for professionals
as good or even better than that of the national government,
and traditions of public service that create an atmosphere
conducive to vigor in administration (Wisconsin is an his-
toric example, New York fits the bill to some extent, and California, also, at least when its top political leadership is not
anti-government in tone), for most of them the need for
technical help is at least as great as it is for money to run
effective programs in this era of professional expertise. Revenue sharing can provide the money, but does not provide
the base or the leverage for extending technical help, either
on a completely voluntary basis or as a quid pro quo for the
provision of aid. In everything from farm programs through
public assistance and highway construction to air and water
pollution control techniques, technical services make the
difference between effective and ineffective expenditure of
funds. In more states than not, there are hundreds of dedi-
cated, programmatically interested civil servants who lack,
however, the professional education and experience that the
better-paid national counterparts possess. Further, no matter
what the salary scales of the states might be, there just
wouldn't be enough top drawer talent trained in each field
to go around. We cannot multiply fifty times the number of
first-rate people in order to have some of them on the payroll of each individual state.

As an example, take the question of curriculum development in the public schools. Education is, at least ideologically, the most local of all governmental functions. Yet the
textbooks used from first grade onward are largely uniform
throughout the nation, being published by national publish-

ers with nation-wide distribution systems. When it comes to developing the best possible textbooks, teaching materials, and conceptual approaches to subjects as diverse as mathematics, foreign languages, and social studies, no local school board can be expected to pull together leading university scholars and outstanding public school teachers from all over the nation to make such efforts. Nor, indeed, can each state be expected to do so. Yet such efforts have been made, with outstanding success, by the School Mathematics Study Group and the Physical Science Study Committee, for example, both of which have been underwritten by the National Science Foundation, an agency of the national government, in cooperation with major universities. Only the national government can pull together the concentrations of talent that these and similar programs have represented, and only the national government is in a position to disseminate the best and latest developments in educational techniques and teaching materials across the whole nation quickly and effectively. The fact that Uncle Sam is really needed [11] is conclusively illustrated by the comment of a 1960 report of the President's Science Advisory Committee which said, in arguing the necessity for federal funds for scientific research in public and private universities throughout the nation, "There is not one physics for California and another for Texas."

Part of the pitch for revenue sharing goes back to the turn-of-the-century notion of the states as experimental laboratories for governmental innovation. In his 1971 revenue sharing message, President Nixon said that revenue sharing would once again enable the states to serve as laboratories for modern government.

Here ideas can be tested more easily than they can on a national scale. Here the results can be assessed, the failures repaired, the successes proven and publicized. Revitalized state and local governments will be able to tap a variety of energies and express a variety of values. Learning from one another and even competing with one another, they will help us develop better ways of governing.

A much more balanced presentation of the case for the states has been made by a former governor of North Carolina, Terry Sanford, in his 1967 book, *Storm Over the States*. After recalling the experimental role of Wisconsin in the years 1900–1914 when the Progressives put into effect there a direct primary, an initiative and referendum, a civil service law, regulatory commissions for transportation and public utilities, state income tax, life insurance and banking regulation acts, child labor laws and conservation laws— truly an astonishing record—he proceeds to argue that "state initiative is not all history." He points to the possibilities of using aerospace technology to solve community problems, an abortive program attempted by former California Governor Edmund G. Brown; New York's far-reaching assault on water pollution under Governor Nelson Rockefeller; the 1963 gubernatorial executive order of Bert T. Combs, Governor of Kentucky, assuring Negroes access to places of public accommodation; prisoner rehabilitation, including a work-release program established in 1913 and copied on the federal level beginning in 1965; community mental health programs, substituting active treatment for custodial care; and California's development of the community college idea.[12] One could add to Sanford's list California's development of air pollution control legislation and administrative programs and Virginia's Department of the Aging. Without doubt, individual states do come up with innovative ideas and do perform useful experimentation.

The problem is: how do you get the rest of the states to

follow suit? The solution is: have the national government adopt the innovation, and with the consultation and advice of the officials who developed it in the initiating state write it into a *mandatory national program* to ensure its dissemination throughout the nation. This is the only way to ensure that the states that most need the innovations will adopt them.

Fiscal poverty and poverty of ideas often go together in state government, especially when the programs are designed to help the least affluent and least influential of citizens—and, the two unfortunately tend to go together—states are loath to spend additional dollars unless compelled to. Sometimes it is not enough for the national government to initiate a grant-in-aid program to stimulate the states on a basis of bribery but without real compulsion. In 1960 an attempt was made in the Kerr-Mills legislation to ward off Medicare. The Kerr-Mills program was one of aid to the medically indigent (Medicaid) and was highly touted by the medical lobby. Unfortunately, by 1965 when Medicare came into being fewer than half of the states had yet opted to join the Kerr-Mills program. Sometimes the carrot needs to be supplemented by the stick: the highway beautification program provides an example. A 1958 statute offered to the states a one per cent bonus on Interstate System highway grants if they controlled outdoor advertisements along the Interstate roads in accord with agreements filed with the Federal Highway Administration. By 1965, only twenty states had entered into bonus agreements and President Johnson changed the system by submitting legislation (quickly enacted) that imposed a 10 per cent penalty on states that did not elect to control outdoor advertising and junkyards in accord with federal standards. As of September 1971 forty-seven states had enacted junkyard compliance laws, and thirty-one had enacted advertising laws, with nine more under active consideration at that time in state legisla-

117

tures. Under the 1965 Highway Beautification Act, Washington was to pay 75 per cent of the cost of sign removal. That went unfunded until 1970; hence, the penalty provisions were suspended until 1971. It takes a lot to get the states to act! [13]

The truth of the matter regarding the notion of the states as experimental laboratories is that it makes a good deal of sense for the initial experimentation, but that the value of the experiments is maximized only if the power of the national government is used to disemminate the successful innovations to all the rest of the states. Relying upon forty-nine state legislatures to learn about the successes of the fiftieth on their own and to institute their own similar programs is to rely on a will-o'-the-wisp. It never did work that way, and it never will. State experimentation combined with national action, ranging variously from the inducement of federal grants through state actions mandated by the national government to directly operated national governments modeled on state experimental programs is the appropriate combination. As was pointed out earlier, after all, the most innovative social experimentation of recent years—the Community Action Programs of the War on Poverty—came from *federal* stimulus, building on some private, foundation-sponsored programs in the juvenile delinquency field.

The matter of state experimentation is related in its assumptions to the myth of state and local governments as being "close to the people." The reader will recall that we quoted President Nixon above as saying that we should "put the money where the needs are" and "the power to spend it where the people are." Following up on this idea in his revenue sharing message, he asserted that state and local officials had unique strengths to bring to bear on problem solving because they "live day in and day out with the results of their decisions." He further said that "because they are closer to the people they serve, State and local officials will often have a fuller sense of appreciation of local perspectives and values."

Let's stop and look at that for a minute. Are they closer to the people? In what sense? What kind of closeness is meant? Closer to all people in their respective jurisdictions, or to certain categories of politically effective people?

Right away, one can point out that for many of the poor, particularly of racial and ethnic minority groups, the dominant state and local figures, both governmental and in the private economic world, are anything but close to the people. The one undeniable consequence of the community action programs, as well as of the civil rights movement with which the war on poverty to some extent merged, was to make the poor and the minorities visible in many communities for the first time—visible in ways that required that state and local officials pay some attention to their needs for the first time. If all of our communities were as homogeneous as are some of the prototypical bedroom suburbs,[14] then closeness of the local political leaders to any segment of the community would give them a fair idea of the needs and values of the whole community. Most cities and counties, and all states, are not that homogeneous, however.

One measure of closeness to the people that easily illustrates that "closeness" in the sense of more information being in the hands of the local citizens does not always correlate with geographic proximity can be gauged by the reader himself. Do you know the name of your city councilman, city manager, county supervisor, state assemblyman, state senator, U.S. congressmen, U.S. senators, governor, lieutenant governor, vice president of the United States, U.S. secretary of the treasury, state finance office head? If you ask these questions of yourself and ten friends—or if a classroom using this book as a textbook surveys itself—I am will-

119

ing to wager that there will be greater recognition of the national than of the local names, on the average. Except for the governor, furthermore, the state level is probably least well known of all. This is a subject on which we are all prone to make off-the-cuff statements, but to which few people have given serious hard thought and analysis. Among the few was the late Morton Grodzins. After suggesting that there are at least six different meanings of "closeness" when applied to governments, he examines some of them in detail. His conclusions are as follows:

(a) Local governments are not closer to the people than is the federal government (or the relevant state government for that matter) as the provider of services. They supply neither all nor the most important local services; nor are they the chief collectors or spenders of public funds. (b) In rural areas the federal government is primarily responsible for supplying local services that for range and impact have no counterpart in the services of any other government anywhere in the nation. (c) If closeness means electoral participation, local governments are further from, not closer to, the people than the federal government. [Compare the voter turnout for a municipal election with the proportion voting for President.] (d) The same statement is true for all localities if closeness means identification. (e) It is almost certainly true in the great metropolitan areas if closeness means understanding of who does what. (f) On the other hand, closeness as directly "taking part" is greatest for rural local governments (largely the result of the high ratio of elected and appointed officers to population), and probably least in the local governments of the great metropolitan areas, with rural participation in federal affairs here occupying some intermediate point. (g) This sort of closeness—i.e., participation—also leads to the personal touch of rural local governments and a hand tooling of service for the recipients, a type of closeness that federally sponsored rural governments also supply to a lesser measure. (h) In many meanings of closeness the differences between urban and rural governments (local and federal) are thus more important than differences between local and federal governments. (i) But in no sense does closeness mean control, and (j) in no sense is closeness exclusively or principally the attribute of local (as opposed to state or federal) governments.[15]

Furthermore, if we are to put the money where the needs are, we would all agree today that the needs are largely in the cities. Will revenue shared with the states reach the cities—as well as, for instance, project grant money presently given directly to local communities in response to locally initiated proposals? The history of state-city relationships is not encouraging. Even when the head of the state government is urban-oriented, the state legislature rarely takes as equally urban-oriented a view as the governor. This is at least one part of the reason for the Rockefeller-Lindsay feud in New York. The historical background had as its central feature the malapportionment of state legislatures with relationship to population. Typically, the lower house was apportioned on the basis of population, but the state senates have often been organized on the basis of one senator for each county, with sometimes extraordinary results. In 1957, for example, Los Angeles County had a population of 4.1 *million* persons while Alpine County in California had at that time a total of 241 persons. To make matters worse, even the state legislative bodies that were legally structured on the basis of population often went twenty or thirty years without reapportionment's taking place even as required by their own state constitutions. Such was the case in Tennessee that led to the landmark Supreme Court decision, *Baker vs Carr*, in 1962, which first established national power behind the "one man—one vote" principle, which was further pinned down for state legislative bodies by *Reynolds* vs

Sims (1964). Where malapportionment has been extreme, it is already helping. But the degree to which it is likely to produce an urban orientation shift should not be overstated in simplistic fashion. Because the major trend in population movement is now toward the suburbs and satellite cities rather than toward the heart of the metropolitan areas, reapportionment on the basis of population trends will shift power more from the rural to the *sub*urban than to the urban areas as such. On the evidence to date, it is unlikely that representatives of upper-middle-class suburbs, populated with people who work in the city but try to escape its problems at night, will have any extraordinary sympathy for the service needs of the central city areas where the poor and the ethnic minorities are congregated. The suspicions of the cities toward the states are by no means a thing of the past.

In fact, the revenue sharing plans have as one of their major "strings" a requirement that each state pass-through some proportion of its shared revenues to all local government units of general purpose, i.e., towns, cities, and counties. Without that requirement, every mayor and county supervisor in the country would have been in opposition to revenue sharing. Even with it, a lot of them are dubious. The Nixon plan of 1971 calls for states to negotiate with their local governments a mutually acceptable formula for passing-through the money. If they could not reach an agreement, then the national government would require a pass-through of that portion of state and local revenues currently raised at the local level in the particular state. On the average, there would be about a 50–50 split between the states and the localities. However, it has been estimated that 67 *per cent* of existing grant-in-aid funds went to metropolitan areas in 1970. It is not surprising that the mayors of fifteen big cities announced that they were opposed to revenue sharing if it were to come by way of cuts in present urban programs. The Model Cities program is in fact one of those scheduled to be eliminated as such, with its functions folded into Nixon's planned special revenue sharing program for urban development.

Recent state experience is not reassuring: it has been reported that anti-crime grants, whose purposes and distribution are defined by state agencies within a federal block grant, were distributed with so little regard for where the needs are that Philadelphia, with 25 per cent of the serious crimes in Pennsylvania, got 10 per cent of the anti-crime planning grants. A careful study of the operation of the Omnibus Crime Control and Safe Streets Act in its first two years found that twelve states had passed-through to their localities more than 75 per cent of the funds required by the Act, but that two-thirds of the states had not awarded the full local share, claiming that the state level programs would be of direct benefit to local jurisdictions. It is doubtful that the local jurisdictions would have agreed. If one uses certain indices of local crime reduction need and effort, then, indicates one report, a majority of states in the first year did not make available commensurate amounts of action funds to their larger localities. Many urban counties did not fare well in the distribution of action monies. A number of the states spread their funds thinly among many small jurisdictions. The report concluded that "a more precise statutory safeguard is needed to ensure that those States which are not already doing so will pinpoint Federal money on areas having the most pressing crime problems." [16]

Pinpointing is the problem. Revenue sharing encourages the frittering away of money in insubstantial amounts, because the politically easiest thing for a state to do is to spread the money evenly in all local jurisdictions, avoiding the hard decisions about where the money is needed most.

123

The national government, perhaps because it is in this respect less "close" to local politics, is better prepared to make these hard choices. Categorical grants-in-aid are administered largely by professionals in each functional field on the basis of professional criteria of need. Shared revenues will be allocated by legislative amateurs or by the less professional functional specialists at the state levels, with much less certainty that the money will in fact go where the needs are greatest. As regards meeting city and county needs through revenue sharing to the states, there is a final and fundamental problem to be mentioned. It is that while one can require a pass-through of money to the localities, there is no enforceable way by which one can ensure that a state does not cut down its other aid to the localities by an amount equal to the shared revenue pass-through. In short, if our major needs are urban needs, we can best be sure that the money goes where the needs are by writing it into the formulas and categories used by the national government in distributing its funds.

In Chapter 3, we argued that the grant-in-aid system shows a healthy recognition that a great many of our domestic problems pertaining to functions within the direct service and purview of state and local governments are now national problems rather than "merely" local. Partly, this is a matter of the economists' doctrine of external economies or spillovers, and partly it is a matter of simply saying that the nationally effective political sentiment of the country sees many matters previously considered to be open to state-local variation as now requiring national uniformity. What is really happening here is that we have become much more of a national community; i.e. we have changed our focus from simply "What do we think as Middletowners?" to "What do we think as Americans?" The most obvious application of these ideas is that if one defines a particular function as national in its implications, then one wants to use the national government to ensure that an adequate minimum standard of service regarding that function is maintained throughout the country. This is the real meaning of the welfare reforms that President Nixon has been advocating, to establish a national floor under public assistance benefits. Increasingly it is also being argued that the national government has an obligation to finance the provision of a national minimum in the per-pupil expenditures on public education, because of the importance of education to the nation, not just to the individual educated or to the town in which he received his early education.

Fundamentally, what is happening is that a nationally effective political majority has reinterpreted the balance of state citizenship and national citizenship, much enlarging the scope of the latter. We no longer are wont to say that what Illinois or Alabama does to its citizens is Illinois' or Alabama's business alone. We are now saying that the resident of either of those states is an American citizen first, and we are very broadly interpreting the Fourteenth Amendment to enlarge his claims against his state. Actually, the Supreme Court, operating outside the framework of immediate electoral constraints or mandates, took the lead in moving us in this direction more than did Presidents or national legislators. Through a long list of civil rights decisions, most notably *Brown* vs *Board of Education* (1954), the "one man—one vote" decisions which interjected national government standards into the internal political structures of the states for the first time, and some recent federal court decisions awarding to public assistance beneficiaries some rights that the states had not previously recognized, the courts have prodded the national conscience.

Once the conscience is prodded, and the new doctrines of national citizenship are disseminated to every corner of the land through the mass media of national circulation magazines and network television, a political majority builds up to carry these doctrines further in the realm of congressionally mandated programs. Grants-in-aid simply provide a major vehicle for establishing national minimum standards in major program areas and for building into federally financed programs that reach the citizen directly through state and local government operations a considerably more enlightened conception of social needs and such basic values as equality of opportunity than would come naturally to most state legislatures or city councils. As we have said more than once in this book, the nationally effective political majority is less status quo oriented than its state counterparts, and the national government's administrative leadership seems to be more capable of resisting narrow pressures than are state administrators.

Perhaps this is partly because, frankly, they are better insulated from the major anti-popular interest groups: the chamber of commerce, realtors' and taxpayers' associations, and dominant manufacturing firms. James Madison, after all, wrote in *The Federalist Papers* that a larger republic was to be preferred to a smaller because no single interest would be as likely to dominate as in a smaller jurisdiction. E. E. Schattschneider has effectively updated the Madisonian doctrine in *The Semi-Sovereign People*,[17] where he argues that the greater the scope of conflict over a decision the more likely is that decision to meet public interest criteria and to be one in which the views of all segments of the community are heard and taken into account.

Unless one is part of that small fringe on the far political right and the far political left that rejects the notions of a national political community, a major—perhaps *the* major —defect of the revenue sharing concept is that it moves us back to the level of separate state political cultures (and to the extent that the pass-through is required, even to the level of separate local political cultures) as the context-setting environment in which public expenditure decisions will be made. In a number of states, the most obvious immediate impact of such a movement would be to return power to state-local officials for whom racial discrimination is still a wholly acceptable premise of public policy. Even with national anti-discrimination statutes (particularly Title VI of the Civil Rights Act of 1964, which permits the cutting off of federal funds from any receiving agency that uses them in discriminatory fashion), could we really feel sure that the values of the national consensus favoring racial equality would prevail over the biased local majorities in the expenditure of federal funds when there no longer would be administrative contact by a national agency supervising the use of the funds in each area, as is presently part of the grant-in-aid system? Because this had been a major objection to revenue sharing on the part of minority group spokesmen, the AFL-CIO, and many other individuals and groups concerned about civil rights as the major national problem, President Nixon made explicit mention of anti-discrimination provisions when presenting his program. His proposed program would forbid any discrimination in activities funded in whole or in part with general revenue sharing funds, and the Secretary of the Treasury would be empowered to enforce this provision. If he was unable to gain voluntary compliance when a violation was found he could then request that the Attorney General seek appropriate relief in the courts or he could begin administrative proceedings under Title VI, looking toward a cut-off of federal funds.

That's fine on paper, but we know that Title VI does not in fact everywhere get enforced with vigor, even in the present system. There is the practical problem already that an agonizing trade-off would sometimes be required: if the funds are being spent on, say, compensatory education programs for disadvantaged students, is it really going to help to cut off the funds because there is some lack of equality in their application? Under general revenue sharing, to this problem would be added the problem that the national government would be much less likely to learn of discriminations as they occur. The Secretary of the Treasury would simply not be in a position (i.e. he would not have any administrative apparatus automatically bringing to his attention the problems) to learn of violations in the same way that officials of the Office of Education or the Urban Renewal Administration or the Farmers' Home Administration are now able to pick up information through the bureaucratic grapevine and through the very processes of reviewing grant applications. The very meaning of our being a federation rather than a confederation, after all, is that in case of conflict between national and state laws, national laws are supposed to prevail. There is, after all, a supremacy clause in the United States Constitution. The advocates of revenue sharing seem to be forgetting that fact.

Other questions apart, there would be more enthusiasm for revenue sharing and much less opposition on the part of supporters of particular grant programs that are already in effect if the latter programs were being funded up to authorized levels. In fact, they are not, and revenue sharing therefore immediately implies a trade-off dilemma: what is spent on revenue sharing cannot be spent on bringing already approved programs up to their authorized levels of expenditure.

The sad fact is that for fiscal 1970 funds actually appropriated for federal grant programs were $8.5 billion *less* than had been authorized for those programs. In percentage terms, appropriations were only 65 per cent of authorizations in fiscal 1970. Worse yet, this authorization-appropriation gap has been growing steadily. In 1966, appropriations constituted 80 per cent of authorizations. Partly this gap is accounted for by very rapid increases in authorizations for certain programs. For example, HEW authorizations increased 137 per cent, 1966–1970, while those for the Department of Transportation (largely the federal aid highway program) increased only 32 per cent. The authorization-appropriation gap is therefore much less in the case of DOT, simply because its authorization has not jumped as much. It thus happens that there is a happier side to the picture: despite the increasing gap, there was a 70 per cent increase in actual outlays in that time period for the grant programs covered in the analysis being used as a basis for these sentences. When outlays for all grant-in-aid programs, including those without fixed authorization, such as public assistance, are considered, we find that the 1966–70 increase was 85 per cent as compared with 47 per cent for the increase in total federal budget.

Because of the structure of Congress, which gives substantive committees responsive to the representatives of particular service needs the responsibility for determining authorizations (which often therefore amount to "what should be" rather than "what can be"), while appropriations are set by committees which are responsible for making ends meet across the board of the national government's budget, we will always have an authorization-appropriation gap. When the gap becomes as wide as it is at present, however, it is clear that the value priorities of the appropriations committees differ substantially from those of the legislative committees. The former, who hold the whip hand, do have an over-all view and an over-all responsibility that the latter lack, it must be admitted. On the other hand, they also tend to be dominated by members from safe districts that are unrepresentative of major national political currents, and they have nothing like the exposure of the legislative committees to presentations about the pressing quality of domestic needs toward which the grant programs are directed.[18] Without going further into the complex questions of the fiscal process in the national legislature, it is clear from this brief review of the gap that those who feel that the national government should be doing more in education, more in community health, more in anti-poverty efforts, more in water pollution control, etc., etc., are going to struggle long and hard to give increased grant appropriations a higher priority than the supplementation of inadequate grants by no-strings-attached revenue sharing to state and local government that cannot be trusted to spend the money for the same objectives. (It is even less likely that Congress will approve the President's proposals to switch much of the money now in the categorical grant form that does establish federal priorities to the form of so-called special revenue sharing that would remove most of the specific priorities.) Having succeeded at the federal level, usually after years of protracted bargaining and political coalition building (i.e. log-rolling), the leaders of major interest groups representing the needs and demands of the schools, the children, the poor, the ethnic minorities, and the cities are not going to accept without a real fight the message that they should now begin over again in all the state capitals. After all, they have focused on Washington in the first place largely because of the proven unresponsiveness of those capitals.

Again, it is a question of which priorities shall prevail, those of the national community or those of the lesser, narrower communities; those of the most inclusive political majority, or those of the most exclusive, status quo dominated pressure systems?

Revenue sharing is thus a cop-out rather than a panacea as far as the responsibility of the national government to

130

make real judgments of its own in response to its own analysis of domestic needs is concerned. There is only one final point to be made now. It is that revenue sharing is also a cop-out as regards the almost universally admitted inadequacies of state and local governmental structure and financial systems. Given the structural inadequacies of weak, short-term governorships, underpaid state legislatures that don't meet often enough, and administrative fragmentation that makes true political accountability impossible in many jurisdictions, Representative Henry Reuss has argued in his very effective little book on revenue sharing that reform of this antiquated and inadequate structure should be an essential prerequisite to the handing over of unrestricted federal funds.

Max Frankel even goes so far as to argue that the Nixon program is "anti-government, hostile to the very idea that the Federal monies and powers should be used to achieve desirable and necessary ends." Granting that present categorical grant programs are often overly restrictive and too much tied up in bureaucratic regulations, Frankel calls it "a long leap backward" to go from there to the notion that national purpose must be abandoned entirely. The President's mistake, he asserts, is that having recognized the inadequacies and inequities of state-local tax systems, he treats those inadequacies and inequities "as if it were beyond the capacity of man and government to change." Instead of using revenue sharing as a lever for change, Frankel charges that the President proposes to underwrite the deplored system indefinitely by not exacting any quid pro quo.

What might that quid pro quo be, concretely? For one thing, a hard-nosed national government that really wanted each state to do all it could for its own citizens would withhold proposed shared revenues from any state that had not yet enacted a personal income tax, which is conceded to be the most effective as well as the most equitable of tax sources. Or the President could sharply penalize in the distribution of shared revenues all states whose total tax take did not equal the proportion of state personal income that was taxed by the average of the top ten states. Why should Connecticut, with very high income and very low taxes, be rewarded for its neglect of the public sector by receiving federal shared revenues in the amount of $59 million, which is one estimate of what that state would receive on a $5 billion revenue sharing plan? [19]

An Alternative Proposal

If revenue sharing is not an appropriate solution to the financial crisis of domestic services, yet we concede that there is a crisis, then what *is* an appropriate response? Is there another way of freeing some state-local funds without giving up the national government's responsibility to define national needs on the basis of its own independent judgment? Is there another way of meeting the valid criticisms about the cumbersomeness and restrictiveness of the categorical grant system? Is there another way of helping the states to help themselves? In each case, I believe the answer is "yes."

The best way for the national government to increase its general financial support of state-local governments while remaining true to its own responsibilities would be to spend its automatic revenue increase of $6 billion or $7 billion annually on the provision of a national minimum standard of service in functions whose importance to the nation is clear or whose handling by state governments has clearly been least satisfactory. Education fits the first criterion, welfare the second. The case for vastly increased national expenditure on public assistance has been made well and forcefully by President Nixon himself and by his former Democratic aide, Patrick Moynihan, who had much to do with the creating of the Family Assistance Plan under which each family of four is to be guaranteed a minimum income of $2400 a year. The federal government might, in fact, well go further: It might take over both the entire financing of public assistance and also the operation of the program. That is, it could "nationalize" public assistance and thus move toward much greater assurance of nation-wide uniformity and equity—not to mention administrative competence—in the delivery of both financial and social services to aided persons.

When this program was absorbed by the national government, the states would be freed of some $7 billion or $8 billion annually in the public assistance share that they would no longer have to provide. That would give them as much as the Nixon general revenue sharing plan had proposed, yet would not involve surrender of national responsibility for the expenditure of national funds.

Once that had been accomplished and even more revenues were available from increased economic growth, the federal government might well move, as is being increasingly suggested, toward the provision of a national minimum educational program for each community. The concept of a basic program in the pre-college years is already well established in the relationship of state governments to local school districts, the states generally guaranteeing a "foundation program" which is then supplemented at the local level through the property tax. A federal minimum educational gurantee of this kind has recently been proposed by economist Richard Ruggles, drawing upon still earlier proposals by Alvin H. Hansen and Harvey S. Perloff.[20] One of the great advantages of national government actions along these lines is that it would make a major contribution toward the equalization of basic human resources services among the states and localities, particularly if the educational foundation program were awarded in the form of per pupil grants to each school district, rather than simply to each state. Yet another candidate for similar treatment is minimum provision for health care for persons of all ages, the obviously logical extension of Medicare for the aged. The vision of national minimum programs in health, education, and public assistance would be a strategy that benefits a nation that has become a single community, and would be well within the anticipated increased revenues of the national government over the next few years. With these basic services largely taken over by Uncle Sam, the state and local governments would be free to concentrate their resources on highways, police and fire protection, natural resources and recreational facilities, and general services.

To maximize what each state could do in these latter realms on its own, the national government should make the adoption of a progressive personal income tax irresistably appealing to all of the states. This it could do by adopting a variant of the tax credit concept which has been advocated by a number of economists (including Walter Heller), by the Committee for Economic Development, and by the Advisory Commission on Intergovernmental Relations. The tax credit works this way: instead of deducting one's state tax payments from one's taxable income on the federal personal income tax return, the individual is permitted to subtract some specified portion of his total state tax bill (a frequent suggestion is up to 40 per cent of his federal tax liability) from his *net federal tax due,* rather than just from taxable income. This would mean a substantial loss of revenues to the national government and indirectly lays a base for a major form of financial aid to the states. The states could, by this system, considerably increase their own rates of taxation at the expense of the federal government rather than at the expense of their own citizens, since an increase in state taxes would be deducted by the taxpayer from his federal taxes, and thus would not be a net increase at all to him, although an increase to the state and a loss to the national government.

I would amend the usual proposals for a tax credit somewhat. Let us permit the credit only for taxpayers of states whose own tax system was reasonably effective—meaning that its personal income tax yielded at least 20 per cent of the federal income tax take in the same state, and that it had some reasonable degree of progressivity in its rates. Also, since the income tax is more equitable than either the property or sales tax, to further encourage its utilization we might permit the tax credit to be taken only for state *income* taxes, with the usual deduction from taxable income continuing to apply to other state taxes (for those itemizing deductions). One further control is needed: to prevent the states from unloading their total service cost onto the national government, there needs to be a limit on the total tax credit permitted. I would imagine that it is not beyond the capability of the economists to determine a percentage of the federal personal income tax take that could be permitted as a credit on the assumption that all states would avail themselves of the possibility of using tax credits. The measures suggested so far would relieve the state and local governments of some of the fiscal pressures, and would encourage them to make greater efforts on their own. It remains to consider what reforms should be made in the grant system to improve its usefulness to the state and local governments and to meet the major criticisms regarding overly narrow categorization and corresponding inflexibility to accommodate to varying needs among the potential recipient governments.

Would the special revenue sharing proposals of President

Nixon accomplish the major objectives here? I think not. They would indeed enhance state-local flexibility, but at too high a price: they would swing the pendulum too far in the other direction. Take the special revenue sharing plan for Urban Community Development as an illustration. In his message to Congress on March 5, 1971, forwarding this program, President Nixon said that the "genius of the Federal system is that it offers a way of combining local energy and local adaptability with national resources and national goals." Since he also said, later on in the same message, that no federal approval would be required in the use of the funds provided by this program, but simply reports periodically on "how the money was expended," it is hard to see just where national goals enter the picture. The urban development plan was proposed to be funded at the $2 billion level in the first year by consolidation of four categorical grant programs previously handled by the Department of Housing and Urban Development: Urban Renewal, Model Cities, water and sewer grants, and loans for the rehabilitation of existing structures. These programs would no longer exist as separate entities. Eighty per cent of the $2 billion resulting fund would be distributed according to a "problem-oriented formula" (i.e. one that takes into account the population in a city, the degree of overcrowding, the condition of housing units, and the proportion of poor families) among each of the Standard Metropolitan Statistical Areas, which are those areas having cities of 50,000 or more population. There are 247 SMSAs. Cities could use their respective shares for investments in both physical and human resource development, including all activities which have previously been eligible for support under the categorical grants that the special revenue sharing fund displaced. Exactly what activities to support and in what proportion are decisions that would be made locally. The remaining 20 per cent of the urban community development money would be used by the Secretary of Housing and Urban Development to compensate communities for reductions in their previous levels of support during the transitional period, and also to perform research, to demonstrate new techniques, and to meet special opportunities—i.e. to use as project grant money is presently used.

The special revenue sharing plans (which in addition to urban community development include the areas of rural community development, education, law enforcement, manpower development, and transportation) appear at first glance to be very similar to the concept of block grants. Block grants, as the reader may recall from Chapter 3, are those which put together a number of the specific categorical grants into a "block" dealing with a particular governmental function, such as education or transportation, and by putting them together in a consolidated pattern permit much greater flexibility for the state and local governing units to receive financial assistance for their particular needs. The Nixon special revenue sharing plans would indeed be like block grants in this respect: they would reduce 130 categorical grants to the six functional areas cited just above. The Nixon plans are quite unlike block grants, however, in some other respects—and the differences do not favor special revenue sharing.

The differences are that the Nixon plans would eliminate existing requirements for matching funds, requirements that receiving governments maintain their own levels of effort and that the expenditure plans be approved by the grant-giving federal agency. By not requiring any matching funds or the maintenance of previous state-local effort, the Nixon Administration is saying that it is perfectly willing to see national revenue sharing used simply as a substitute for state-local revenues, rather than making a real effort to see that it is itself additive and that it stimulates additional state-local effort. It might help a President and some Congressmen get re-elected by easing the state-local tax burden in the short run, but it would do so at the expense of making any added contribution to the solution of domestic problems. By abandoning the requirement of project approval by the granting agency, the special revenue sharing plans remove a sense of national goals almost as effectively as would general revenue sharing. It is one thing to allow each receiving jurisdiction to work out a program on its own initiative; it is quite another to award federal funds without the slightest review of the adequacy and legitimacy of those programs. Like general revenue sharing, special revenue sharing thus designed would be a large step backward in the development of American federalism. We are more and more a national community; doesn't it make sense that we should more and more go by our *national* judgment of priorities among social needs?

We are not, incidentally, without some evidence on the problems that would arise if we simply gave large chunks of money out to the states and localities and said spend it on education or spend it on rural development. Title I of the Elementary and Secondary Education Act of 1965 (ESEA) was, in its original form, akin to a block grant in that the means by which each school district would attempt to reach the objective were totally unspecified, although the purpose was clearly specified to be improvement of the education of children of poverty families. Audits of Title I projects made by the Department of Health, Education and Welfare show, for example, that $2 million to $3 million were used in South Carolina for investment in classrooms and libraries for segregated schools for blacks, facilities which white schools in the state had funded out of local funds. A Mississippi high school spent its Title I funds on twelve television sets, tape recorders and filmstrip projectors for every two or three classrooms, dictaphones, calculators and adding machines, electric typewriters, a deep-fryer, sheet music and choir robes, a bedroom suite for the home economics department, and a china cupboard. While some of these things may indeed have helped students, it is rather doubtful that they were all oriented specifically toward the needs of the poverty children in the school.[21] Another program that was designed as a block grant, the 1968 Crime Control and Safe Streets Act, has also had its problems in trusting to the sense of priorities of the receiving officials. In Alabama, it was revealed early in 1971, it was alleged that most of a $200,000 police officer education grant was converted into college scholarships for sons of the bigwigs in the public safety department.[22]

In addition to the good substantive reasons why revenue sharing should not be adopted, the efforts on its behalf are wasted because we can predict rather confidently that it will not be adopted, or would not last if it were adopted. I would like to see us move somewhat in the direction of block grants—although I would reverse the Administration's system and give 80 per cent of the funds in a functional area by approval of grants and only 20 per cent on a formula basis that would permit free experimentation by the receiving jurisdiction (but the facts of the matter are that the Congress has steadily moved away from block grants even in the small number of cases where it has started out with them). As has already been mentioned, the Partnership in Health Program, the Omnibus Crime and Safe Streets Act of 1970, the Community Action Programs of OEO, and Title I of ESEA have all gone through a similar function and a specific purpose but did not mandate the particular application of the funds, and each has undergone year-by-year amendments of a continually more restrictive nature, spelling out the particular ways in which Congress wants to see the money spent. The 1969 OEO authorization, for example, allocated $328 million for "local initiative programs" (i.e. the original, innovation-enhancing Community Action Prgrams), but then imposed Congress's own program priority choices by specifying that $890 million would be reserved for work and training programs; $398 million for the popular Head Start Program; $58 million for legal services; $8 million for the Senior Opportunities and Services Program, and so forth.[23] This is, of course, the reason why we have the categorical grant system to begin with. It is not that congressmen are unaware of the problems associated with proliferation of 500 different categories, but that they would consciously prefer to pay the price in administrative complexity in order to obtain the gain in specificity of national goals in the present system.

In conclusion, a pattern that would reflect political realities and the sense of values contained in the national community would be to expand and improve upon the existing grant-in-aid system by closing some of the gap between authorizations and appropriations, by further consolidating the handling of related project proposals as has been done under the Model Cities Program while still retaining the requirement of federal approval,[24] by freeing perhaps 10 to 20 per cent (at the most) of categorical grant money in each major category in each major function for experiments at the discretion of the states, and by further developing the administrative improvements contained in the Intergovernmental Cooperation Act of 1968 and those proposed since, such as delegation of project approvals to field officers and further training of local government personnel. Further, increased federal revenues should be used to provide equalized national minimum programs in public assistance, education, and medical care; and, finally, greater state use of the personal income tax should be stimulated by adoption of a federal tax credit. This "package" of reforms would maintain, I believe, an appropriate balance between national values and varying state-local needs.

The revenue-sharing concept has been useful, even though it should not be adopted. It points up the inadequacies of state-local government structures and state-local financial systems, and it forces us to clarify our own ideas about the development of the United States as a national community, with all the implications that that notion possesses for the changing meaning of federalism.

III

Prognosis and Prescription

5

In Praise of Permissive
Federalism

It is time now to ask ourselves: What have we established through our review of fiscal federalism, the grant-in-aid system, and revenue sharing schemes? If one had to make a single summary statement in reply, it might be that federal financial aid for purposes selected by the national legislature has created a *nationally dominated system of shared power and shared functions.* Extensive movement toward the revenue sharing alternative would shift the pattern toward a state-dominated system of shared functions. In either case, it is clear that the basic relationship between the nation and the states today, whatever the theory or practice of federalism may have been earlier, is one of *inter*dependence rather than *in*dependence. Furthermore, the interdependence is one of mutual leverage so far as power relations are concerned: although the national government is basically dominant, the states and localities retain sufficient political strength to ensure that their views will be listened to by the national government in designing its programs, and that they will have considerable discretion in the implementation of programs that are federally funded.

Now let's look at these elements in greater detail. First of all, why do I say that the system is nationally dominated? When one looks at the resistance power of state and local governments, and at the choices available to them as regards which project grants to participate in, it might seem that they are in the driver's seat, rather than Uncle Sam. However, the picture changes sharply if we compare the present system with that which we would obtain under revenue sharing. In comparative terms, there can be no doubt: categorical grants and the few block grants that presently exist comprise a system in which the basic program choices in the expenditure of federal funds are clearly made on a national priorities basis.

Another comparison is also relevant. If we compare the reach of the federal government today with that which existed prior to World War II, one would have to say that the range of public sector decisions subject to national government influence is immeasurably greater now. It is not just that the national government enters into domestic affairs much more than was the case in earlier days, but that the standards it sets in the areas where it directly makes decisions affect also the climate within which similar decisions are made by state and local governments. For example, the existence of merit system requirements in federally aided programs puts pressure on spoils system states to modify their practices in programs not aided with federal funds. At the least, the existence of higher standards in federally aided programs provides leverage in the form of an arguing point for those trying to establish higher standards in unaided programs.

That is to say, when we speak of a nationally dominated governmental system, we do not mean that the national government makes all the decisions so much as that it now greatly affects many decisions it does not make. This spillover effect could hardly operate as a strong factor unless something else had occurred of a quite intangible nature; namely, a much broader acceptance of the national government's legitimacy than was the norm when the states' rights conception of federalism held sway over most of the nation. Actually, acceptance of national government priorities in grant-in-aid programs is only one manifestation of this enhanced legitimacy of Washington in domestic affairs. As suggested earlier in this book, both court decisions and non-financial legislation in areas of civil rights, legislative apportionment, voting rights, and the establishment of air and water anti-pollution requirements are now largely taken for granted, but less than a generation ago would have been considered severe violations of the vulgarized Tenth Amendment form of federalism. The eighteen-year-old vote is a good illustration of the sea change that has occurred in our expectations regarding federalism. When Congress passed legislation giving eighteen-year-olds the right to vote in national elections there was some question as to whether the Supreme Court would uphold this assertion of national authority. It did, and without any general outcry. Now, that has been quickly followed by the ratification of a constitutional amendment extending the eighteen-year-old vote to all elections. Thus does another previously exclusive area of state jurisdiction—control over elections—topple before the notion that the United States constitutes a single national community.

Political life is complex, however. Having established that our over-all system is now nationally dominated in the senses indicated, we need to point up the qualification that the dominance is often greater in potential than in actuality, and that it co-exists with a great deal of autonomy on the part of the states and localities—even with victories by the lower jurisdictions in specific instances. The dependence of national political authority upon a heavily decentralized party system, as Grodzins has stressed, has a good deal to do with this mutuality of leverage. For example, when the U.S. Department of Health, Education and Welfare attempted in 1965 to withhold funds from the city of Chicago because of questions about that city's compliance with federal requirements, the political clout of Mayor Daley within the Democratic party brought a quick resumption of funding. Even apart from the party system's influence, however, there would be substantial power on the part of state and local governments in the discretionary implementation of federally aided programs simply because of the fact of interdependence and the one practical administrative consequence of formal federalism—the inability of federal officials to fire recalcitrant state or local government employees.

Where conflicting interests and values are at stake—as they always are in public policy—few questions are settled "on the merits" since the merits themselves are part of what is in question. Power and influence depend on persuasion, it's true, but persuasiveness is considerably enhanced when the persuader has some sanctions over the one he is attempting to persuade. Anyone who has authority to fire me can count on my listening attentively to his thoughts and preferences. Since this kind of authority relationship over personnel within an organization is the ultimate sanction underlying all lesser sanctions, its absence from the relationship between federal grantors and state-local grantees considerably dilutes the reach of the former. Even within a single organization where this sanction does exist, we have learned through the theory of informal organization— especially from the seminal writings of Chester I. Barnard [1] —that authority is much more elusive than the simplistic notion of one man being in a position to give orders to another. An executive has authority over the employees to the extent that they accept his right to direct their behavior, that is, to the extent that they consider his claim to authority to be "legitimate," which in turn may rest upon their view regarding whether he has a claim to their allegiance on the basis of superior expertise, or superior knowledge of the situation, or simply legal power. If authority in an organization that does possess hiring and firing powers nevertheless rests upon the consent of the governed, then all the more so does the achievement of federal purposes in the aided programs depend upon the willing cooperation of the grantee governments. And they are unlikely to concede either a theoretical legitimacy to the "Washington bureaucrats" as they will see them, or the legitimacy of superior knowledge, since they will see themselves as having a monopoly on knowledge of the particular local situation.

The futility of trying to make generalized answers to questions about the distribution of national power is demonstrated by yet another qualification that we need to make at this point, namely, that what we have been saying about state-local leverage applies mostly to formula grants, much less so to project grants. In formula grants, the burden of proof is on the national government to show that there is good reason to withhold what the law automatically grants on the basis of certain minimal general conditions. When a project grant is at stake, however, the burden of proof shifts to the proposing state or local agency for it must make a positive showing that it warrants the grant requested on the basis of a proposal superior to those of competing applicants. Another way of putting it would be that formula grants are given "of right," while project grants represent "a privilege." As the proportion of project grants grows (and for fiscal 1970 the dollar total of federal project grant obligations was equal that of formula grant obligations), state-local influence will find one of its supports weakening. As we have said, of course this is not the only source of state-local influence, although it is a very important one at the level of particular decisions involving particular communities. At the more general level of state-local participation in the development of the general outlines of national programs—specifically including their influence in seeing that new national programs are developed within the grant-in-aid context rather than becoming direct operations of the central government, I would expect that source of influence to remain as vigorous as ever for the foreseeable future. Whether loosely structured, undisciplined, locally oriented political parties are cause or consequence of constitutional formalities of federalism (and whichever came first the relationship appears to be one of symbiosis now), the effect of both is to give a much more localized tone to so-called national programs than would otherwise be the case. Grodzins states the matter well:

> The political potency of the local organization has a very important effect on national policy. In at least one sense, it makes a counterweight against the tendency to centralize power in Washington. The history of legislation with respect to many important programs . . . shows national legislators writing national legislation with a sensitive ear to state and local political leaders. This is a natural tendency in the light of political realities: The American national legislator considers himself the representative of district and state interests because its position is secured through the efforts of state and district—not national—political organizations.
>
> The politics of administration is a process of making peace with legislators who for the most part consider themselves the guardians of local interests. The political role of administrators therefore contributes to the power of states and localities in national programs.[2]

In addition to all of the factors above that qualify national dominance, there is another that operates even in the absence of state-local demands. It is buck-passing by the national government. The reader may recall that Philip Monypenny explains the whole grant-in-aid system as a compromise based on the fact that interest groups wanting certain government actions are sometimes strong enough to move the Congress in the desired direction while not unified sufficiently to demand an integrated, directly national program. The other side of this coin is that the national legislature, in the words of Martha Derthick, uses the grant system

. . . to enable the federal legislature to commit itself to serving very broad national purposes (such as "more adequate" welfare) without assuming the burden of making all of the political choices it would have to make in a unitary system (how much welfare, for whom?). The difficult choices may be left to other governments.

She adds that the vitality of the American Congress in comparison with the legislatures of other nations "may be attributed partly to the opportunities the federal system provides for responding to pressures for action while limiting the risks of the response." [3]

It has long been noted in the literature on government regulation of business that the independent regulatory commissions (e.g. Federal Communications Commission, Interstate Commerce Commission, Federal Power Commission, etc.) operate at a considerable political disadvantage vis-à-vis the interests they are supposed to regulate because the organic statutes under which they operate are so vague as to the goals and standards that they are to enforce. That is to say, the Congressional mandates are vague—such as the requirement that the FCC allocate radio and television frequencies on the basis of "the public interest, necessity, and convenience," whatever that may be. This is legislative buck-passing, because the Congress is not simply being reticent; rather, it is reflecting its own lack of consensus. It knows only that it wants to regulate, but cannot agree on how much regulation. It therefore gives a blank check of undetermined value, as it were, to the administrative agency. In similar fashion, much grant-in-aid legislation reflects the presence of a Congressional consensus that action should be taken in a particular sphere, and equally the absence of a Congressional consensus regarding exactly what that action should be or how much action. Again, as Derthick points out, to formulate precise and internally consistent policies is always difficult but "grant programs may magnify the difficulties because the extremely diverse interests of all state governments are directly engaged in the programs' operation." [4]

What Are the Trends?

The section immediately above attempts to sketch the situation as of today. Now it is time to ask: What are the predictable trends in the further evolution of the system? First of all, it seems safe to say that the states and localities will become even more dependent upon federal financial assistance in the next few years than they already are. The service demands that a growing population and urban complexity make upon these governments cannot but increase, and more than proportionately to the rate of population growth. Public sector services constitute a major and increasing portion of the American standard of living, and as Gross National Product rises so do our expectations for public services, including importantly those that are needed for the full enjoyment of related private expenditures.

For example, the more we spend on putting a second car

in each suburban family, the more we need to spend on highways, traffic signals, policemen, and traffic court judges. The more money we have in our pockets privately, the more we go on vacation, and when we go on vacation we make ever greater use of public facilities. Visitors to the national park system increased from approximately 130 million in 1969 to 170 million in 1970 and topped 200 million in 1971. To camp overnight in one of California's state beach parks on the Pacific Ocean requires making a reservation for July or August in January or February.

To the assertion that the federal financial role in the inter-governmental system will increase further there are two qualifications to be made. First, part of that increase will take the indirect form of federal tax credits for state income taxes. I say this because it seems clear that the debate over revenue sharing has brought the inadequacies of state-local tax effort into public view to such an extent that there will have to be a reform response. The near-unanimous consensus among intergovernmental fiscal experts seems to be that the states could considerably increase their own revenues if they all adopted income taxes and extended those taxes to higher progressive rates—perhaps even making all state income taxes a percentage of federal income taxes paid. This won't happen without federal prodding, however. To the extent that the federal government succeeds with the carrot of tax credits, it is of course subsidizing the state tax systems to the extent that the credits exceed the state tax deductions already imbedded in the federal income tax system. That subsidy will not show up in the figures on grants-in-aid, however. A second way in which the domestic role of the national government will increase without affecting fiscal federal statistics as such lies in the assumption by the national government of services previously handled on a shared basis or not included in the public sector at all. I have reference here, of course, to the assumption of welfare costs by Washington, but also to the very clearly predictable extension of public medical care financing from the aged to the entire population.

Because of both ideology and the structure of political power as indicated above (i.e., a structure that often enables interest groups to obtain program authorization at the national level while leaving the hard decisions about exact program content to the state level), however, the domestic public services will continue to be handled on a sharing basis, both fiscally and operationally. If there ever was a time of separated functions (which it seems to this writer that there once was to a considerable extent, despite the Grodzins-Elazar contentions to the contrary), as the dual federalist proponents have always assumed, then those days are gone forever. The only way that functions will be separated by level of government in the future will be by the federal government taking over entirely (for purposes of ensuring even-handed administration) certain services previously performed on a shared basis. And that's not exactly what the voices crying in the wilderness for a revised states' rights federalism have in mind.

The third prediction—and I think it a very safe bet—is that the predominant mode of federal financial assistance will continue to be that of categorical grants, with some attempts at consolidation looking toward block grants. Revenue sharing, in the true sense of funds supplied without programmatic strings of any kind, is not likely to amount to much, if indeed it is enacted at all. We may indeed end up with some old wine in apparently new bottles, which will be a little bit confusing but which will not really change the situation. That is, if something like President Nixon's special revenue sharing plans are enacted, it will be with a number of strings attached right from the beginning—as is already apparent from a review of the plans as presented to Congress even before sufficient amendment had been accomplished to build the coalitions necessary for passage. And within a couple of years of passage, so many additional restrictions would be added, particularly by way of requiring federal approval of the specific areas in which the money is spent, that what may be called revenue sharing will at the most be block grants. On this point there cannot really be any doubt. Every time Congress begins with a broad grant of authority, it ends up, as we have seen, changing that broad grant into a series of specific grants as it receives feedback information on uses of the funds that it finds are politically popular and those that cause political trouble. And after all, isn't this programmatically as well as politically sensible?

At the beginning, one may want sufficient experimentation to find out what approach to a problem works best. Once one gets some comparative experience from a number of localities—using the states as experimental laboratories but with federal funds—then would it not be foolish to continue the unfettered freedom rather than to specify that the method proven most successful be adopted by all jurisdictions?

Finally, my expectation in the broadest terms is that the fundamental trend in the development of our intergovernmental system will be a continued further development of the notion of a national community, and further continued ideological acceptance of the corollary proposition that it is proper for the goals and standards of public services to be set by the national government as a basis for uniform rights of citizens no matter where they live. Perhaps the prevailing idea was once to accept as appropriate differentials in services between states on the simple basis that a person was a citizen of one state or another and it was up to each state to

155

determine what level of services it wanted to provide. In that conception, I have no complaint if, living in Arkansas or Vermont, my children's education may suffer from a less than minimal per pupil expenditure level, while those who happen to reside in California or Massachusetts or New York enjoy superior education simply by being citizens of another state.

Increasingly, I am arguing, we are coming to define certain basic services as "rights" of national citizenship, and among these services are education, medical care, and public assistance for the poor. In a sense, it may be that the civil rights movement and the Supreme Court's response to it in the form of fleshing out the Fourteenth Amendment have performed a great service for *all* citizens by compelling us to confront more than we ever had before the value choices inherent in the distinction between asserting the primacy of state citizenship and that of national citizenship. Equality before the law, as guaranteed by the Fourteenth Amendment, is confined in the terms of that Amendment to certain specific kinds of discrimination; but by analogy it is being extended broadly to equality of social services regardless of geographic location within the country. Combined with the general cultural homogenization occurring through the media of communications and the ease of transportation, this trend means the end of much of the social diversity that is the only logical basis for continuation of old style federalism in the sense of acceding to the different value norms of different geographic areas.

What Does Federalism Mean Now?

The Constitution has been properly described as a living document, one whose provisions must be reinterpreted in each age lest there develop an unbridgeable "generation gap" between the founding fathers and the electorate of the present day. Because we accept substantive changes more easily when they can be covered by the old labels—thus permitting us to fool ourselves a little bit into thinking that change is less than it really is—we are likely to go on using the word federalism with content greatly changed. However, if we are going to continue to use the old label, we had better be explicit with ourselves about what it no longer means; we had better reiterate briefly what federalism is *not*.

Among the things that federalism does *not* mean today are:

1. A constitutionally fixed distribution of functions between the two levels of government.
2. Separation of functions such that there are no overlaps in jurisdiction among the levels of government.
3. Reservation of certain spheres of authority in the states that cannot be touched by the national government.
4. Financial independence on the part of the states.
5. A relationship of coordinate equality between the states and the central government.
6. That the Tenth Amendment provides any obstacle whatsoever to the further extension of the authority of the national government.

Federalism, in short, is not like the Iron Curtain or the Berlin Wall: it is not something that makes a high barrier between the actions of the national and state governments, nor something that has its essence in a competitive relationship. Is there any sense, then, in which federalism remains a constitutional concept? It is not any longer a legal aspect of the system as regards distribution of power between the central and regional governments, for that is now a matter of policy rather than legality, given the breadth of Supreme Court interpretation of the relevant constitutional clauses.

157

There is, however, one sense in which the constitutional meaning of federalism still has importance. That lies in the guaranteed independent existence of the states. Because the boundaries of a state cannot be changed without its own consent, and that is unlikely to be given, even the prescribed formal mechanism for constitutional emendment cannot eliminate a state against its wishes. This fact in itself may not seem to have great significance, but one corollary does: the fact that the state appoints its own officials. If ours were a unitary state, then at least in theory there is no reason why all civil servants throughout the country might not be appointees of the central government and therefore removable by that government. Under federalism, the jobs of state and local officials derive not from the national but the state capitals, and though the federal government may finance all or part of the salaries of state and local officials and may establish requirements in its grant programs regarding the manner of their appointment, it cannot directly hire or fire them. Because the states do have this one kind of formal autonomy, formal federalism does indirectly maintain a base for local political strength: since political parties revolve around offices, and states provide offices to be filled by election rather than by national government appointments, constitutional federalism does provide a continuing base for some measure of decentralization in the party system. That it requires the present degree of decentralization seems to be doubtful, but I will not go into that. This autonomy of personnel, both elective and appointive, is *the* remaining significant fact arising out of the constitutional formalities of federalism. All else of the so-called principles of federalism is so much rhetoric today.

The difference between old style and new style federalism could be summed up this way: Old style federalism described a non-relationship between the national and state governments. New style federalism refers to a multifaceted positive relationship of shared action. The meaning of federalism today lies in a process of joint action, not in a matter of legal status. It lies not in what governments are, but in what they do. It is a matter of action rather than structure. It is dynamic and changing, not static and constant. What federalism in the form of the politics of intergovernmental relations amounts to today from the viewpoint of the states and localities is (1) a right to be heard in the design of programs and (2) a right to share in the implementation of programs. If the generic part of the concept of federalism lies in the notion that the parts have a say in shaping action, as well as the center that represents the whole, then federalism is as alive today as in the time of James Madison. On the other hand, if one defines federalism this broadly it becomes almost synonymous with democracy. Why is that? Because in any system that is democratic, whether formally unitary or federalist, the people and their organizations will have an opportunity to be heard, both through the vote and through parliamentary discussion. It is because this is so that Great Britain has a long tradition of very vital local government despite its unitary constitutional structure. And, as the Soviet Union and any of a number of South American republics illustrate, a country that is not democratic can be ruled arbitrarily from the center despite the clearest kind of constitutional provisions embodying federalism.

What is essential to free government is not formal federalism, but First Amendment freedoms—those of speech, press, and assembly—and the right to organize groups and petition the government, and the right to vote. These outlets for whatever pluralism of ideas and interests and values exists in the society constitute the essence of freedom. Institutional patterns do not determine relationships of power, but reflect them. That our system of government retains great flexibility in the relationship between the national government and its citizens, and great openness to influence by the citizenry, is easily illustrated when we consider the growth of new modes of local influence, modes that have more than made up for any loss of local strength resulting from the demise of constitutional federalism. The new modes I refer to are "direct federalism" (referring to national-city relationships that bypass state governments) and "private federalism" or "federalism by contract" (relationships by which non-governmental firms and groups of all kinds perform the government's business under grant or contract). The latter is the essence of what former President Johnson's Administration was fond of calling "creative federalism." Together, direct and private federalism constitute very significant symbols of the liveliness and strength of social forces outside of Washington.

The Models Revisited

It is time now to take a backward glance at the adequacy of well-known conceptions of federalism in the light of the *Realpolitik* of grants-in-aid and the intergovernmental relations picture that most of this book has been about. The first thing that our analysis does is to back up with the evidence of administrative experience the theoretical formulation popularized by Morton Grodzins under the label of "marble cake federalism." While not by any means the only way in which the federal government shares functions and authority with state and local governments, grants-in-aid are certainly "where the action is" today. The quality of federalism (in the sense of sharing power between central and regional jurisdictions) is, I think, much more vitally affected by sharing that involves intimate day-by-day association, as do all grants-in-aid but particularly project grants, than by those instances of sharing that are discrete and discontinuous, such as the simultaneous existence of both federal and state legislation affecting elections or the party system or the sporadic connections involved in federal court review of state court judgments.

At the same time, however, Grodzins perhaps carried the implications of his analogy farther than was justified. In his various writings on federalism, including his posthumous book, *The American System*, there is an implication, I feel, that proof that the states were involved in activities jointly with the national government proved also the continuing vitality and strength of state government vis-à-vis the national government. That is to say, he may to some extent have confused sharing of functions with sharing of power. Because he was very much a pluralist (i.e. a believer that the national interest could be defined as the action that resulted from the free interplay of competing groups), he stressed as a matter of value as well as simply fact the force of localism in the American party system and at least implicitly suggested that this force would keep the national government from dominating the marble cake. Grodzins's posthumous book was published in 1966, and the editing had been finished the previous summer. Grodzins died in 1964, just before the explosive proliferation of grant programs, particularly those of a project nature with fairly tight requirements for federal approval. While his conception of sharing still holds up as a major corrective to the older image of dual federalism with its pretense that national government stayed out of most domestic areas that state and local governments were engaged in, it is itself an inadequate conception as regards the delineation of the intergovernmental relationship in terms of the thrust of power and the answer to the question, Who decides what the priorities will be?

Both the dual federalist conception and the extremely legalistic and formal criteria for testing the presence of federalism set forth by K. C. Wheare can be rejected as pictures of the American intergovernmental system. Dual federalism, the reader may recall, was the term used by the late Professor Edward S. Corwin to capture the flavor of the late nineteenth- and early twentieth-century period in which the Supreme Court interpreted the American Constitution as requiring a hands-off relationship between state and national governments. The national government was not to regulate many matters—such as child labor or industrial safety—because these were presumed to lie within the area of jurisdiction reserved to the states or to the people by the Tenth Amendment and not (as later came to be the case) open to national action on the basis of a broad interpretation of the commerce clause; while the states were for a time forbidden to act in the same areas on the grounds that to do so was to take property without due process or to interfere with liberty of contract. That kind of federalism created a no-man's-land in which neither level of government could act, let alone think about joint action. Wheare's litmus test for federalism includes a requirement that the regional governments be financially independent of the central government, which we have clearly seen that they are not; he also requires that the power relationship be such as to justify the adjective "coordinate," as distinguished from superordinate and subordinate. As we remarked at the outset, that is not the case.

Ever since the constitutional revolution of 1937, the nation-state relationship has been seen as predominantly one of "cooperative federalism," meaning at the least that where the national government has not acted the states are generally free to act, so that we are not without government at all in some areas as was the case for a time under dual federalism. And at the most cooperative federalism means some-thing close to the marble cake conception of *simultaneous* national and state action in the same sphere. So far as it goes, cooperative federalism is still an accurate enough label, as was the Johnsonian sequel, "creative federalism," as a shorthand way of referring to the development of adminis-trative relationships in which the national government uses non-governmental bodies as administrative entities to carry out its programs. What neither of these says anything about, however, is the question of who dominates in a partnership or cooperative arrangement.

The latest attempt at labeling the system for the purposes of both description and prescription is President Nixon's "New Federalism." As we saw in the chapters on revenue sharing, the essence of the so-called New Federalism is in fact the reactionary (in the literal sense) notion of moving back toward a day when there were no national priorities, when there was no particular content to the concept of na-tional citizenship, when to speak of one's "community" usually meant one's home town, and perhaps sometimes one's state, but never the United States as an integrated na-tional entity. The New Federalism is, in short, simply ro-mantic rhetoric, a façade behind which the national govern-ment is to abrogate its domestic role, to reduce its presence merely to that of an onlooker—or a fairy godmother who will provide the wherewithal for Cinderella (in the form of state and local governments) to achieve whatever her wishes may be.

I propose a new label. (I might as well play the game too.) Mine is "permissive federalism." The notion that phrase conveys (I hope) is that there is a sharing of power and authority between the national and state governments, but that the state's share rests upon the permission and per-missiveness of the national government. The broadness or specificity of congressional grant legislation measures in each instance the degree of national consensus versus state and local diversity that exists with regard to the subject matter of that particular legislation. The legal authority to impose whatever degree of restrictiveness it wishes exists unquestionably in the national government. It should be clear at once that this is not federalism at all in the classic conception. Federalism in that sense is dead. We have at last become one nation, indivisible, and if justice for all is to be achieved it will not be by leaving its definition to the dominant factions of small areas. James Madison was, after all, right: the larger the area and diversity of populations encompassed in a governmental jurisdiction, the less the chance that any one faction will ride roughshod over others. We were, however, too diverse and socially pluralistic for a long time to permit the results even of pluralistic politics to result in national action. We have now achieved that degree of unity and can express a national consensus in at least some areas and to some degree, a consensus that does not represent the final victory of any one elite or any one interest, but the embodiment of difficult-to-arrive-at coalition agreements.

Is Permissive Federalism Good?

To state that the system is one of permissive federalism is to state a fact and not an evaluation. Is it a good thing, or something to be regretted? That is our final question. I think the careful reader of the preceding pages will know my answer: In this writer's opinion a system of shared functions and shared power under federal leadership and within the boundaries set by whatever priorities a national consensus is able to agree upon is very much the right thing. We no longer need the constitutional pluralism of the dual federalism type. Granted that there are still some regional diversities and perhaps even differences in state cultures, these can be sufficiently accommodated within the boundaries of implementation of permissive federalism; they do not require the abstention of the national government from domestic affairs. Actually, James Madison was almost too right in his prediction that government in the larger area would prevent domination by a single interest: it almost prevents any resolution at all of a public interest. Our problem may not be (as President Nixon apparently believes) that the national government has become too powerful while state and local governments are weak and atrophied; it may be instead that the national government is only now beginning to achieve the amount of power needed to govern effectively. At least one political scientist has argued provocatively and well that the national government has allowed far too much of its own programs to be shaped by unaccountable local governments and local non-governmental groups. Theodore J. Lowi, in *The End of Liberalism,* attacks what he calls "interest-group liberalism" as a vulgarization of pluralism that "renders government impotent." In his view, "liberal leaders do not wield the authority of democratic government with the resoluteness of men certain of the legitimacy of their positions, the integrity of their institutions, or the justness of the programs they serve." [5] As an example, Lowi discusses at some length the War on Poverty of the Johnson Administration and argues that the Economic Opportunity Act of 1964 represented a total abnegation of the federal government's responsibilities because it failed to define a conception of poverty; it failed to define a methodology for attacking poverty; and in its most innovative feature, that of the Community Action Programs, it was simply an open-ended invitation for local groups to define their own policy regarding poverty. The Community Action Programs, he argued, were completely "process-oriented," and lacking all substantive guidance for either the head administrators in Washington or the local grant-receiving groups in the cities. In Lowi's view, interest group liberalism, which is the dominant political ideology of the United States at the present time, insists upon overdoing the notion of representation at points where it is inappropriate. That is, it confuses representation with administration, and in so doing makes it impossible for the government to give firm definition to policy at the top. To provide representation down at the bottom is to let policy be made at the bottom. In his view, this is decentralization run riot: "A time when national standards and local realities are almost completely out of joint is hardly a time for decentralization." [6]

Personally, I think that Lowi is a little too harsh in his evaluation. While it is undoubtedly true that delegation of program-defining and to some extent policy-defining power to local groups on occasion means that the shape of local initiatives will be contrary to national policy (as in the instance of a southern city's plans for segregated urban renewal, plans which were accepted by the federal agency), and at other times the locally initiated programs will simply be ineffective and a waste of money, it is also true—which I think he fails to give due weight to—that on still other occasions good ideas will be brought forward which might not have occurred to the program leadership in Washington. Innovation is hard to come by in public policy, and it is worth some risk and some price in misdirected or ineffective efforts. Regardless of whether one agrees with Lowi's evaluation or not, however, it is hard to argue with his factual analysis of the situation. He provides very good evidence and argument in support of his proposition that policy making in many of the newer domestic programs *is* already very heavily decentralized because of the present

166

passion for participatory democracy in the administration of programs. And if Lowi is correct, then President Nixon and many other devotees of revenue sharing are not correct as regards the present balance between national and state-local power.

Permissive federalism is good, I conclude, exactly because it can strengthen the national government by permitting firm national definitions of policy objectives and program approaches at the same time that it can make all the room needed for appropriate state-local inputs to the details of program implementation. Permissive federalism is, in fact, the effective key to administrative decentralization, because such decentralization makes sense and is safe from the viewpoint of accountability only when it is within the boundaries and constraints set by firmly developed policy at the top. Dual federalism was wrong because it encouraged a false competition between state and national governments and left too many problems in a no-man's-land in between. Cooperative federalism was an improvement, because it presumed that there would always be room for some government to act, and it encouraged the levels to act jointly on occasion. But it was inadequate conceptually because it tended to assume that the responsibilities of state and national governments were coordinate, whereas the reality is that the national government needs to be superior. Its cooperation with the states should always be on the basis of national standards rather than adjusting its scales to state-local standards, which in many instances would be below those of the national government.

Permissive federalism provides the blend appropriate to the 'seventies. By the 'eighties, who knows? Maybe then we will finally feel enough of a national community to permit ourselves to be a unitary state in name as well as in fact. The founding fathers were willing to change the style of government from the Articles of Confederation to the Constitution of 1787 when it became clear that different times demanded different rules of governance. Should we be less bold than they?

Notes

1 IS FEDERALISM DEAD?

1. William H. Riker, *Federalism* (Boston: Little, Brown, 1964).
2. Grodzins's major work, which was posthumous, edited by Daniel J. Elazar, is *The American System* (Chicago: Rand, McNally, 1966).
3. Daniel J. Elazar, *The American Partnership* (Chicago: University of Chicago Press, 1962).
4. "The Federal System," in President's Commission on National Goals, *Goals for Americans* (Englewood Cliffs, N.J.: Prentice-Hall, 1960).
5. K. C. Wheare, *Federalism* (New York: Oxford University Press, 3rd edition, 1953).
6. Ibid. p. 53.
7. *U.S.* vs. *Darby*, 312*U.S.* 100, 1941.
8. *U.S.* vs. *Butler*, 297*U.S.* 1.
9. M. J. C. Vile, *The Structure of American Federalism* (New York: Oxford University Press, 1961), pp. 3, 65.
10. William Anderson, *The Nation and the States* (Minneapolis: University of Minnesota Press, 1955), pp. 135–36.
11. William H. Young, *Ogg and Ray's Introduction to American Government* (New York: Appleton-Century-Crofts, 13th edition, 1966), p. 65.
12. John H. Ferguson and Dean E. McHenry, *The American*

System *of Government* (New York: McGraw-Hill, 8th edition, 1965), pp. 87, 89.

13. Charles R. Adrian and Charles Press, *The American Political Process* (New York: McGraw-Hill, 2d edition, 1969), pp. 109, 144.
14. Emmette S. Redford, David B. Truman, Alan F. Westin, and Robert C. Wood, *Politics and Government in the United States* (New York: Harcourt, Brace, 2d edition, 1968), pp. 68, 103, 93.
15. James M. Burns and Jack W. Peltason, *Government by the People* (Englewood Cliffs, N.J.: Prentice-Hall, 6th edition, 1966), p. 99.
16. Gaylon L. Caldwell and Robert M. Lawrence, *American Government Today* (New York: Norton, rev. edition, 1969), p. 67.
17. William Ebenstein, C. Herman Pritchett, Henry A. Turner, Dean Mann, *American Democracy in World Perspective* (New York: Harper and Row, 1967), pp. 175, 176.
18. Robert K. Carr, Marver H. Bernstein, and Walter F. Murphy, *American Democracy* (New York: Holt, Rinehart & Winston, 5th edition, 1968), p. 61.
19. Adrian and Press, op. cit. p. 157.
20. On dual federalism generally, see Edward S. Corwin, *The Twilight of the Supreme Court* (New Haven: Yale University Press, 1934), Ch. 1, and his article, "The Passing of Dual Federalism," *Virginia Law Review*, Vol. 36 (1950).
21. 247 U.S. 251 (1918).
22. See Theodore J. Lowi, *The End of Liberalism* (New York: Norton, 1969).
23. Carr, Bernstein, and Murphy, op. cit. p. 56.
24. Quoted in Aaron Wildavsky (Ed.), *American Federalism in Perspective* (Boston: Little, Brown, 1967), pp. 37, 36.
25. Both arguments may be found in Wildavsky, ibid.
26. Vile, op. cit. p. 39.

2 THE CRISIS OF FISCAL FEDERALISM

1. Walter W. Heller, *New Dimensions of Political Economy* (Cambridge: Harvard University Press, 1967), p. 129.

2. Ibid., pp. 121–22.
3. J. K. Galbraith, *The Affluent Society* (Boston: Houghton Mifflin, 1958), p. 263.
4. U.S., Office of Management and Budget, *Special Analyses, Budget of the United States Government, Fiscal Year 1972,* p. 239.
5. Henry S. Reuss, *Revenue-Sharing: Crutch or Catalyst for State and Local Governments?* (New York: Praeger, 1970), p. 25.
6. L. L. Ecker-Racz, *The Politics and Economics of State-Local Finance* (Englewood Cliffs, N.J.: Prentice-Hall, 1970), p. 39.
7. Reuss, op. cit. p. 27.
8. Ibid. p. 26.
9. Ecker-Racz, op. cit., pp. 202, 77.
10. See Advisory Commission in Intergovernmental Relations, *Measuring the Fiscal Capacity and Effort of State and Local Areas* (Washington, D.C., March 1971), p. 209.
11. Ecker-Racz, op. cit. p. 210.
12. From Tax Foundation figures quoted in "The States Tackle Tax Problems," *New York Times,* 27 June 1971, Sec. F, p. 13.
13. Ecker-Racz, op. cit. p. 20.
14. Heller, *New Dimensions of Political Economy,* p. 131.
15. *U.S. News and World Report,* 7 June 1971, p. 59.
16. Sources: Frederic C. Mosher and Orville F. Poland, *The Costs of American Governments* (New York: Dodd, Mead, 1964); U.S. Bureau of the Census, *Census of Governments, 1967,* and U.S. Bureau of the Census, *Governmental Finances in 1968–69* (GF 69, No. 5). The same sources were used for Table 2.
17. Source: U.S. Bureau of the Census, *Governmental Finances in 1967–68.*

3 *GRANTS-IN-AID: THE CUTTING EDGE OF INTERGOVERNMENTAL RELATIONS*

1. *Ogg and Ray's Introduction to American Government,* p. 62.
2. Letter, L. Richard Gabler of Advisory Commission on Intergovernmental Relations to the author, 29 June 1971, based on an office of Management and Budget study.

3. See Bureau of Outdoor Recreation, U.S. Department of the Interior, *Federal Outdoor Recreation Programs* (Washington, D.C.: G.P.O., 1970).

4. Advisory Commission on Intergovernmental Relations, *Fiscal Balance in the American Federal System*, Vol. 1 (Washington, D.C.: G.P.O., 1967), p. 153.

5. Message to Congress on Special Revenue Sharing for Urban Community Development, Press Release, 5 March 1971.

6. Letter to author from Samuel L. Becker, Acting Director, Division of Mental Health Service Programs, National Institute of Mental Health, U.S. Department of Health, Education and Welfare, 18 August 1971.

7. W. Brooks Graves, *Intergovernmental Relations* (New York: Scribners, 1964), p. 546.

8. E. E. Schattschneider, *The Semi-Sovereign People* (New York: Holt, Rinehart & Winston, 1961).

9. For a relatively brief yet authoritative presentation of the external benefits justification for grants-in-aid, see George F. Break, *Intergovernmental Fiscal Relations* (Washington, D.C.: Brookings, 1967), Chapter 3.

10. National Science Board, *Toward a Public Policy for Graduate Education in the Sciences* (Washington, D.C.: National Science Foundation, 1969), pp. 37–38.

11. Phillip Monypenny, "Federal Grants-in-Aid to State Governments: A Political Analysis," *National Tax Journal*, Volume 13 (March 1960), pp. 1–16.

12. Advisory Commission on Intergovernmental Relations, *Fiscal Balance in the American Federal System*, Volume I, p. 149.

13. James L. Sundquist, *Making Federalism Work* (Washington, D.C.: Brookings, 1969), p. 127.

14. Commission on Intergovernmental Relations, *Report* (Washington, D.C.: G.P.O., 1955), p. 64.

15. These quotations and the discussion in which they are embedded are found in Sundquist, op. cit. pp. 3–6.

16. William Anderson, *The Nation and the States*, p. 213.

17. Walter Lippmann, *The Public Philosophy* (London: Hamish Hamilton, 1955), p. 44.

18. Break, op. cit. p. 95.

19. *Fiscal Balance,* Volume I, p. 153.

4 REVENUE SHARING—PANACEA OR COP-OUT?

1. Walter W. Heller, "Should the Government Share Its Tax Take?" *Saturday Review* (22 March, 1969), pp. 26–29.
2. Ibid.
3. W. W. Heller, *New Dimensions of Political Economy* (Cambridge: Harvard University Press, 1966), pp. 168–69.
4. W. W. Heller, Richard Ruggles, et al., *Revenue Sharing and the City* (Baltimore: Johns Hopkins University Press, 1968), p. 35.
5. From a column by Harley L. Lutz in the *Wall Street Journal*, 12 December 1966, reprinted in *Revenue Sharing and Its Alternatives: What Future for Fiscal Federalism?*, U.S. Congress, Joint Economic Committee, Joint Committee Print, 90th Congress, 1st Session, 1967, Volume 2, p. 937.
6. From Mills's speech of 26 January 1971, as printed in *Congressional Record*, Volume 117, 92d Congress, 1st Session, 26 January 1971, p. H210ff.
7. Martha Derthick, *The Influence of Federal Grants* (Cambridge: Harvard University Press, 1970). See also Gilbert Y. Steiner, *Social Insecurity* (Chicago: Rand McNally, 1966), for a strongly put statement of the extent of which Uncle Sam has been *too* willing to forgo calling the tune, despite continually paying a large share of the piper's cost.
8. See David O. Porter and David C. Warner, "How Effective Are Grantor Controls?: The Case of Federal Aid to Education," in Kenneth Boulding (ed.), *Transfers in an Urbanized Economy* (Belmont, Calif.: Wadsworth, forthcoming).
9. See Charles R. Adrian, "State and Local Government Participation in the Design and Administration of Intergovernmental Programs," *The Annals* (of the American Academy of Political and Social Science), Volume 359 (May 1965), pp. 35–43.
10. Christopher Jencks, "Why Bail Out the States?" *The New Republic* (12 December 1964), pp. 8–10.
11. See Michael D. Reagan, "Uncle Sam Is Really Needed," *New York Times Magazine* (13 September 1964), p. 31ff.
12. Terry Sanford, *Storm Over the States* (New York: McGraw-Hill, 1967) Chapter 7.

13. Letter to the author, 1 September 1971, from Michael Lash, Director of Environmental Quality, Federal Highway Administration, U.S. Department of Transportation.
14. See Robert C. Wood's classic study of the homogeneous suburb and its closed-in qualities, *Suburbia* (Boston: Houghton Mifflin, 1958).
15. Morton Grodzins, *The American System*, edited by Daniel J. Elazar (Chicago: Rand McNally, 1966), pp. 210–11.
16. *Making the Safe Streets Act Work: An Intergovernmental Challenge* (Washington, D.C.: Advisory Commission on Intergovernmental Relations, 1970), p. 62.
17. E. E. Schattschneider, *The Semi-Sovereign People* (New York: Holt, Rinehart, 1961).
18. On the composition and operating characteristics of the appropriations committees, see Richard F. Fenno, Jr., *The Power of the Purse: Appropriations Politics in Congress* (Boston: Little, Brown, 1966).
19. Max Frankel, "Revenue Sharing Is a Counterrevolution," *The New York Times Magazine* (25 April 1971), p. 28ff.
20. See Ruggles's remarks in Walter W. Heller, Richard Ruggles, *et al.*, *Revenue Sharing and the City*, pp. 39–72.
21. For these and further gruesome details, see *Is It Helping Poor Children?*, a report by the Washington Research Project (NAACP Legal Defense and Education Fund, Inc., 1969).
22. Based on an editorial in the Riverside, California *Press*, 26 February 1971.
23. *Public Law*, pp. 91–177, 30 December 1969.
24. As special revenue sharing began to founder in Congress in the summer of 1971, the Nixon Administration moved in this direction incrementally by announcing a system called "planned variations," which is intended to give mayors with Model Cities grants greater flexibility and authority in the allocation of federal aid. See *New York Times*, 7 November 1971, I, p. 74.

5 *IN PRAISE OF PERMISSIVE FEDERALISM*

1. Chester I. Barnard, *The Functions of the Executive* (Cambridge: Harvard University Press, 1938).

2. Grodzins, *The American System,* pp. 376–78.
3. Derthick, *The Influence of Federal Grants,* p. 196.
4. Ibid. p. 195.
5. Theodore J. Lowi, *The End of Liberalism* (New York: Norton, 1969), p. 288.
6. Ibid. pp. 226–39, 268.